An Introduction to Education Studies

Also available from Continuum

Comparative and International Education, David Philips,
   Michele Schweisfurth and Erwin Epstein

Exploring Key Issues in Education, Dean Garrett and Derek Kassem

Key Issues in Secondary Education, John Beck and Mary Earl

An Introduction to the Study of Education, Jane Bates and Sue Lewis

Perspectives on Participation and Inclusion, Suanne Gibson and Joanna Haynes

Philosophy of Education, Richard Pring

Psychology and the Teacher, Dennis Child

Reflective Teaching 3rd Edition, Andrew Pollard

A Sociology of Educating, Roland Meighan, Clive Harber, Len Barton,
   Iram Siraj-Blatchford and Stephen Walker

Symbolic Clothing in Schools, Dianne Gereluk

Theory of Education, David Turner

An Introduction to Education Studies

The Student Guide to Themes and Contexts

Edited by

Sue Warren

continuum

Continuum International Publishing Group

The Tower Building	80 Maiden Lane
11 York Road	Suite 704
London SE1 7NX	New York NY 10038

www.continuumbooks.com

British Library Cataloguing-in-Publication Data
A catalogue record for this book is available from the British Library.

ISBN: 978-0-8264-9919-6 (hardcover)
      978-0-8264-9920-2 (paperback)

Library of Congress Cataloging-in-Publication Data
An introduction to Education studies : the student guide to themes and contexts / edited by Sue Warren.
      p. cm.   Includes index.
   ISBN: 978-0-8264-9919-6 (hardcover)
   ISBN: 978-0-8264-9920-2 (pbk.)
1. Education. 2. Education–Philosophy. 3. Education–Aims and objectives.
I. Warren, Sue. II. Title.

LB1025.3.E3346 2008
370—dc22

2008034524

Typeset by Newgen Imaging Systems Pvt Ltd, Chennai, India
Printed and bound in Great Britain by the MPG Books Group

Contents

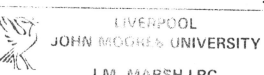

List of Contributors

Brendan Bartram is Senior Lecturer in Education Studies at the University of Wolverhampton

Bridget Cooper is Reader in Education at Leeds Metropolitan University

Les Hankin is the Associate Director of Widening Participation at Liverpool Hope University

Colin Harrison is a Senior Lecturer and the Education Studies Course Leader at Leeds Metropolitan University

Pat Hughes is a Senior Lecturer in Education at Liverpool Hope University

Julian MacDougall is Reader in Media and Education and Head of Creative Arts at Newman College of Higher Education, Birmingham

Barbara Murphy is a Senior Lecturer in Education and a Teaching Fellow at Bishop Grossteste University College, Lincoln

Jon E C Tan is a Senior Lecturer in Education and the Professional Doctorate in Education Course Leader at Leeds Metropolitan University

David Trotman is Head of Education Studies at Newman College of Higher Education, Birmingham

Gary Walker is a Senior Lecturer in Childhood and Early Years at Leeds Metropolitan University

Susan Waltham is a Senior Lecturer in Childhood and Early Years at Leeds Metropolitan University and the BA (Hons) Childhood Studies Course Leader

Sue Warren is the Education Subject Group Leader and Principal Lecturer in Education Studies at Leeds Metropolitan University

Margaret Wood is a Senior Lecturer in Education at York St John University

Acknowledgements

The editor would like to thank the contributing authors without whom this book would not have come about; Jo Allcock and Ania Leslie-Wujastyk at Continuum for their support; Iain Poole for the compilation of the index.

Introduction to Education as a Field of Study

Sue Warren

Chapter Outline

Introduction

Everyone has their own definition of what education is based on their own experiences of schools and colleges. Beginning university is seen as a continuation of this seamless flow for students embarking on degree courses. Some might define education as a process whereby knowledge is learnt and skills developed; a simple enough description of individual lived experiences. For some this educational process has been enjoyable and enlightening, for others it will have been constraining and not particularly worthwhile. Whichever, a trawl of people in the community at large will find views across this continuum. What, then, is the nature of education as an academic journey?

This book has been written for students beginning their study of education. The intentions of the authors are to engage students in thinking about and interacting with complex themes through the use of the disciplines and perspectives which underpin Education Studies courses. Students will be encouraged to engage in activities and readings to investigate a range of contexts in the landscape of education.

The book is structured into two parts: Part I themes; Part II contexts. Part I introduces some of the major themes in the study of education and Part II explores the contexts within which education happens in order to stimulate consideration of education in action.

Education as a field of study

What do students study in education studies degrees?

Courses leading to education(al) studies degrees can be seen to be made up of modules of study in disciplines such as the philosophy of education, comparative education, the history of education, sociology of education, psychology, global education, health education and so on based on the Quality Assurance Agency (QAA) *Subject Benchmarks for Education Studies* (QAA, 2007).

Activity 1.1

Look at six university prospectus entries for Education(al) Studies degrees on the internet.

What do the course outlines state that students will study?

Are some fields of study more common than others?

Can you sense whether some fields of study seem to be more important than others? Which? Why?

When embarking on the academic study of education students will be asked questions such as:

- What is education? (A process or a product?)
- What is knowledge? (Do various types of knowledge have different status?)
- What are the purposes of education? (Control or enlightenment? Who decides?)
- Where does education happen?

In trying to answer, or pose, such types of questions several disciplines such as those above will be drawn upon.

The UNISEF Convention on the Rights of the Child states that every child should have the right to education. It does not lay down what that education should be, when it should start or when it should end. Each individual country which signed up to the Convention will have its own views, comparative education studies these differences (see Bartram in this volume). Since the turn of the century, UNESCO has been active in the continuing development of education, setting goals for their *Education for All by 2015* policy.

Activity 1.2

Access the UN Millennium Development Goals website and read about the education goals for 2015 and the progress being made towards their achievement.
www.un.org/millenniumgoals

Access the New Partnership for Africa's Development and the European Union websites to find out what the goals are for education in these groups?
www.nepad.org/2005/files/home.php and www.ec.europa.eu/education/policyareas/education

How do the goals of the three organizations match? What are the differences? What do you think may be the reasons for these differences?

Education as a contested term – philosophical approaches

The meaning of the word 'education' has been contested since the times of the Ancient Greek philosophers. Philosophical approaches to the study of education interrogate the meaning of the conceptual nature of the term. Carr (2005: 45), debating the relationships between philosophy and education, states that without a knowledge and understanding of the historical development of philosophy the question of the relationships cannot be answered and Sewell and Newman (2006: 5) maintain that 'the term "education" is not an easy one to define, often being wrapped up with ideas of "schooling," "learning" and "training."'

Peters, a seminal philosopher of the twentieth century, asks in his introduction to *Ethics and Education* (1966) what the philosophy of education should be concerned with, giving four major points for debate:

- 'the analysis of concepts specific to education'
- 'the application of ethics and social philosophy of education to assumptions about justification for assumptions about desirability of the means of transmission, problems of procedure which raise ethical issues to do with liberty, equality, authority and punishment'
- 'empirical questions about learning and motivation, about conceptual schemes of psychology and how these assumptions can be tested'
- 'problems related to the curriculum' (Peters, 1966: 18, 19)

For him morality, intentionality and worthwhileness are the key aspects of education.

Activity 1.3

Read:
1. Sewell and Newman's chapter, 'What is education?' in Sharp, Ward and Hankin (2006) *Education Studies an Issues-based Approach*.
2. Matheson's chapter, 'What is education?' in Matheson (ed.) (1999) *An Introduction to the Study of Education*.

Make notes on their discussions.

How do these authors answer the same question?

Education purposes and aims – politico-ideology approach

In the late nineteenth century, Queen Victoria commanded Lord Russell, the Leader of the Privy Council, to write a letter to Lord Lansdown expressing her desire that the State become engaged in educating the populace due to 'a deep concern [about] the want of instruction which is still observable among the poorer classes of Her subjects' laying down a curriculum of 'Religious Instruction, General Instruction, Moral Training and Habits of Industry' (Lord John Russell, 4 February 1839, in Maclure, 1965). Why was the time right for the State to become involved in what had previously been the arena of the Churches (established and non-conformist) and philanthropists? How did the influences of the expansion of the British Empire, the rapid industrialization in Britain and the political unrest in France underpin this? Through the study of the history of education, ideologies and political changes, the importance of maintaining the status quo of the class system, of creating a literate workforce and coping with the expanding growth of the Civil Service, the imperialist and economic aspirations of the ruling classes can be seen. This is an example of a functionalist ideology in which the maintenance of the status quo, social and cultural norms through a curriculum based on what is seen to be worthwhile knowledge attuned to the status of the learners in order to continue the growth and prosperity of the nation with respect to economic and political power is a driving force.

The Marxist ideological stance would not support this. Marxists see the holding of power by the state in the hands of an elite as wrong and here would follow a conflict ideological approach whereby education would be contested in detail to challenge the power of the State for the good of the populace. A liberal ideological approach would see education as the means by which the education of individuals could be a means to change society. The social justice ideological approach would draw on knowledge thought to be desirable for encouraging changes in society based on a critical analysis of social injustices.

The ways in which policy decisions are made and implemented reflect the ruling political party's ideological stance.

Activity 1.4

Find out about the Thatcherite ideology of the market place.

How did this ideology shape the way in which school management changed in the 1980s?

How is this different to the New Left's ideological basis for educational policies between 1997 and 2008?

Education and sociological perspectives

Education can be looked at through several sociological lenses, for example, gender, social class, race and ethnicity. The ways in which curricula, policies, knowledge status are influenced and/or defined from different sociological perspectives can be viewed from different sociological perspectives. Thus, it can be seen that the sociology of education itself is underpinned by a variety of perspectives. Ball claims that 'the sociology of education has its own sociology [with a predominantly] Western [standpoint], European and Anglo-Saxon philosophical traditions, to all intents and purposes, define the sociology of education.' (Ball, 2004: 2). The interplay of ideological, cultural, economic factors weigh heavily in discussions about, for example, curriculum development (Kelly, 2004), influences on self-image of learners from different class background (Reay, 2004), gender (Meighan and Harber, 2007). Tan and Harrison use such an interplay of sociological lenses in their chapter in this volume.

Part I: Themes in the study of education

It can be seen then that Education Studies degrees draw on a range of subject disciplines, for example, history of education, philosophy of education, sociology, comparative education and so on. By using the term 'themes', the authors in this book explore how these various disciplines can be used either as a single focus or jointly in ways which interact in the exploration of a range of aspects of education.

Educational theory

MacDougall and Trotman (Chapter 2) offer an approach to the development of intellectual skills in the study of education and as such provide a diagnostic introduction for students new to the study of the field. They explain clearly the distinction between the study of education, training to teach, and developing reflective educational practice and judgement in a range of situated practices and professions. It then supports work in the first of these areas and examine the relationship with the latter.

The chapter sets out a clear set of criteria for 'theorizing' the study of education to help students make the transition from reflective discussion of their own educational experiences (and their opinions) to debating educational issues from informed perspectives. The paradigms covered include the established traditions that are typically drawn on for key concepts – sociology, psychology and philosophy of education – and also the range of emerging discourses around theoretical work on the imagination, representation and cultural questions related to educational technologies.

The interrogation and comparison of contemporary global issues

Bartram (Chapter 3) provides students with an introduction to the fields and discipline of comparative education. This chapter includes an examination of the historical evolution of the subject from the nineteenth century until the present day, where interest in comparative research is often driven by political concerns about educational standards, academic achievement and economic competitiveness. Bertram develops a discussion of the various aims and purposes which have been attached to the discipline, giving an analysis of the problems and issues faced by those involved in comparative educational enquiry. Particular attention is paid to the importance of looking at educational issues in their social context, and the problems of "uncritical transfer", that is, the adoption of educational practices from elsewhere without due regard for the contextual factors that are often responsible for their 'local' success.

Students are provided with an overview of the key areas and themes of enquiry in the field, and activities which offer opportunities to use analytical frameworks for comparing education systems or exploring educational issues in a comparative context.

Ethical issues in education

Waltham and Warren (Chapter 4) explore the ethical dimensions of education and educating. The chapter begins by exploring the philosophical background to ethics looking at Platonic and Socratic underpinnings to modern concerns about ethics following World War II. The influences of the Nuremburg Trials on medical ethics are explored. The authors discuss the differences between ethics and morals and global and national examples of ethics in action are considered. Researching with children and vulnerable adults in educational settings are discussed with respect to the rights of research participants and the giving of consent to participate, for example. Ethical considerations of the responsibilities of educators are thus raised.

The application of different sociological lenses

Tan and Harrison (Chapter 5) use the theme of an educational autobiography of 'Philip' as a tool by which sociological impacts on an individual's experience of education can be explored. By viewing Philip's educational autobiography analytically through different lenses a range of concepts and issues are raised and explored in a way which problematize the relationships among aspects of social class, race/ethnicity and gender. Students are asked to think about how aspects of Philip's educational career can be conceptualized and accounted for in exploring educational experiences through these lenses both individually and collectively. Tan and Harrison provide students of education studies with skills and concepts through which to challenge how the education system is organized, how political decisions based on attempts to measure difference influence decision-making and government policies.

Affective issues in education

Cooper (Chapter 6) draws on recent and current work in the field of affective issues in education. Students are invited to interrogate how developments in the areas of neuroscience and how the brain functions have led to an increase in the knowledge and understanding of the intrinsic nature of emotions in educational processes. Looking at the relationships between philosophical and scientific constructs, the focus is on the significance of educational transactions between learners and educators. The ways in which the education system places constraints on the ability of teachers, the educational environment and its management to raise the importance of empathetic ways of working are explored and implications for best practice suggested.

Part II: Contexts for education

Authors in Part II of this book explore educational themes as they are lived in formal and informal, compulsory and non-compulsory educational contexts to encourage students to consider how educators work as education changes, for example, in the light of policy changes to "wrap around" care and education Extended Schools, Children's Centres and the recent Children Plan (DCSF, 2008); changes to curriculum and also in lifelong learning contexts. The role of other professionals working with educators in educational contexts is also explored.

Breaking barriers to learning through the range of professionals working together in schools

Hughes (Chapter 7) uses the theme of a school journey in which a tour around a primary school shows a range of professionals working in the school alongside the teachers since the publication of *Raising Standards and Tackling Workload* (DfES, 2003) and *Every Child Matters* (DfES, 2004). Hughes organizes the chapter to discuss those who are employed by school, the local authority, public services or who are volunteers. The roles and responsibilities of learning mentors, higher level teaching assistants (employed by school); behaviour management unit worker, parent mentor, extended school workers or Children's Centre workers employed by Local Authorities (LA) or commissioned by LA; school nurse, social worker (employed by health and social services); governor, parent helper (volunteers) are discussed. Students are asked to consider the implications for the changing role of the teacher, the need for new leadership and management skills and the greater awareness of the growth of multi-agency working in schools.

Safeguarding children and adults in educational settings

Walker (Chapter 8) briefly covers the current frameworks and guidance, along with underpinning key principles and philosophy, which govern the safeguarding of both children and adults. The Children Act 1989 and the subsequent three versions of the accompanying guidance on *Working Together to Safeguard Children* (DfES, 2006), the Children Act 2004, the Safeguarding Vulnerable Groups Act 2006 and the Protection of Vulnerable Adults Scheme are introduced.

In relation to children, he examines the inconsistencies and complexities in this legislative framework, including in such areas as the definitions of child abuse. The move away from narrow 'protection' towards one of 'safeguarding and promoting the welfare of children' is explored. Current trends and their inherent tensions are critically analysed, for example, the continuum of 'child in need' to 'child in need of protection', or the move to early intervention and prevention. For both children and adults alike, the extent to which the term 'safeguarding' is agreed and understood by all is addressed, alongside other terms such as 'vulnerable'. Walker discusses some of the fundamental questions this analysis raises, for example, about the relationship between individuals, the family and the state, or about the desire to eradicate risk.

Social and educational responses to disaffection

Murphy (Chapter 9) explores three key aspects of disaffection within education. She examines perceptions, issues and ideas regarding the nature and causes of learner disaffection, with particular reference to the English compulsory education system through a critical examination of recent social, cultural and educational changes. The impact that these changes may exert on the learner, in terms of their experiences within the classroom and their expectations of their role within society, is considered. In the second section of this chapter, Murphy considers how disaffection may present itself in the classroom, with specific reference to self-esteem, behaviour, truancy and exclusion using recent research concerning pupil's perceptions and experiences of disaffection.

The effects of contemporary local, school and government initiatives and strategies that aim to address learner disaffection are analysed with reference to the taught curriculum and the effect of improved choice to learner attitude. Finally, Murphy explores the effectiveness of whole school systems for the management of behaviour and the role of community and parental involvement.

Giving pupils a voice in their education

Wood (Chapter 10) considers the place of learners' voices in their education arguing that children and young people's voices should be taken into account and given status. By interrogating the background of policy changes leading to the raising of children and young people's voices and drawing on her own work, Wood explores two British examples of how secondary schools have encouraged students to engage in their schools' development. The first example shows how students were involved in a Making Learning Better project at their school, the second relates to engaging students in research not as participants but as active researchers.

Wood finally turns to a discussion of the international implications and processes for learners' voices to be heard in policy developments across the globe.

Education beyond schools

Hankin (Chapter 11) introduces evolutions in lifelong learning, learning beyond the traditional compulsory schooling system, maintaining that the shifting boundaries that this implies are evidence of the changing nature and concept of 'Education'. Giving a brief outline of the historical developments in lifelong learning, Hankin explores how the Widening Participation agenda has grown as the government responds to global, economic and social mobility trends thus creating a series of impacts on education.

The changes in the knowledge society which are seen in the expansion and 'massification' of Higher Education across the globe leading to changes in what is seen as Higher Education is critically analysed as a paradox of expansion versus the choices made by individuals. The contested nature of the aims and purposes of education for a narrowing of opportunities between 'learning opportunity and social capital' are explored.

Conclusion

This chapter has introduced readers to the themes and contexts which are discussed and developed in more detail in the following chapters.

Summary

- education can be viewed through a variety of perspectives
- education as a field of study draws on approaches related to perspectives of philosophy, political ideologies, sociology
- introduction to the following chapters

References

Ball, S J (ed.) (2004) *The RoutledgeFalmer Reader in Sociology of Education.* London: RoutledgeFalmer

Carr (2005) *Making Sense of Education: An Introduction to the Philosophy and Theory of Education and Teaching.* London: RoutledgeFalmer

DCSF (2008) www.dcsf.gov.uk/publications/childrensplan/

DfES (2003) *Raising Standards and Tackling Workload.* Nottingham: DfES Publications

DfES (2004) *Every Child Matters: Change for Children in Schools.* Nottingham: DfES Publications

DfES (2006) *Working Together to Safeguard Children: A Guide to Inter-agency Working to Safeguard and Promote the Welfare of Children.* Norwich: The Stationery Office

Kelly, A V (2004) *The Curriculum Theory and Practice* (5th edn). London: Sage

Maclure, J S (1965) *Educational Documents England and Wales, 1816 to the Present Day.* London: Methuen

Matheson, D (1999) (ed.) *An Introduction to the Study of Education* (2nd edn). London: David Fulton

Meighan, R and Harber, C (2007) *A Sociology of Educating.* London: Continuum

Peters, R S (1966) *Ethics and Education.* London: George Allen & Unwin

Quality Assurance Agency (2007) *Subject Benchmarks for Education Studies* (QAA, 2007)

Reay, D (2004) 'Finding or losing yourself? Working-class relationships to education', in Ball, S J (ed.), *The RoutledgeFalmer Reader in Sociology of Education.* London: RoutledgeFalmer

Sewell, K and Newman, S (2006) 'What is education?' in Sharp, J, Ward, S and Hankin, L (eds), *Education Studies: An Issues-based Approach.* Exeter: Learning Matters

Sharp, J, Ward, S and Hankin, L (2006) (eds), *Education Studies: An Issues-based Approach.* Exeter: Learning Matters

UNICEF (2006) *Convention on the Rights of the Child.* www.unicef.org.crc/ (accessed 14 March 2008)

Further reading

Barlett, S and Burton, D (2007) *Introduction to Education Studies* (2nd edn). London: Sage

Kassam, D, Mufti, E and Robinson, J (2006) (eds), *Educational Studies: Issues and Critical Perspectives.* London: Open University Press

Mufti, E, Kassam, D, Murphy, L and Naylor, A (2008) *Educational Studies: An Introduction to Key Issues.* London: Open University Press

Useful websites

www.dcsf.gov.uk – Department for Children, Schools and Families. On this site you will find leading work across government in England to improve outcomes for children, including policies related to education, children's health and child poverty for example.

www.dius.gov.uk – Department for Industry, Universities and Skills. Use this site to investigate how education in the post-compulsory sector works.

www.nepad.org/2005/files/home.php – New Partnership for Africa's Development. Here you will find policies related to improving the education of children in the participating African countries.

www.ec.europa.eu/education/policyareas/education – On this site you will find the European Union's (EU) educational policy and documents related to it. Links will take you to the individual countries in the EU and their national education policies.

www.un.org/milleniumgoals – In 2000, the United Nations developed a set of goals to be met by member nations by 2015. The goals for education and reports of projects to date can be found on this site.

Useful internet search terms

education

educational philosophy

educational policies

education and politics

educational sociology

comparative education

ethics in educational research

emotional intelligence

safeguarding children

disaffection

children's voices

lifelong learning

Part I
Themes in the Study of Education

'Doing Theory' on Education

Julian MacDougall and David Trotman

Chapter Outline

Education Studies will mess with your mind!

(Katie, Education Studies undergraduate student – advice to undergraduate students as they were about to enter the world of Education Studies for the first time).

Why theorize education?

Students are understandably tense about embarking on a three-year degree in a subject that does not actually exist in schools or further education. As a former Education Studies undergraduate, Katie was in a good position to know this. Her comment certainly received a few laughs during student induction, but, moreover, it established a really important point early on: Education Studies is *supposed to* mess with your mind. Through making the *familiar* world of education – after all, students are *in* education at the same time as studying it – *unfamiliar* it is possible to take a step back and look at it as an idea, a practice and even a form of control.

Because we have all experienced education, the subject is profoundly different to, say, Maths. Although a mathematician would say quite rightly that the universe is understood by human beings pretty much totally in mathematical patterns and structures in one way or another (whether most of us realize this or not), mathematics cannot be discussed in relation to everyday life experience in the same way as education can. Most people can offer an opinion straight away in response to something like discipline in schools or the value of a University degree, but it is a bit harder to offer a perspective on relativity or chaos theory. This makes it vital to always theorize education, to ensure that what students are doing is sufficiently informed by research, discussion, argument and a range of academic reading. To state very simply, it is a good idea for students to regularly review their work and ask themselves – could someone who is *not* skilled in the study of Education at degree level understand this? If the answer is yes, then students are probably not 'doing theory' enough.

So this theoretical distancing of oneself from education allows the student to interrogate it, to explore and to question it – why do we have schools, why do we fail people, why are governments so obsessed with changing education all the time, why is the school curriculum in England organized around subjects and why is education so important in prisons? These are some questions that one can only start to answer if time is spent labouring over facts, opinions, research and personal experiences. Putting a range of ideas together, testing how they fit or contrast, reflecting on how they relate to one's own experiences and how individuals are culturally 'situated' within education – this is 'doing theory'. And the 'doing' word is very important. Theory has connotations of being dry, abstract, artificial when set against the more lively, applied 'real world' notion of its 'sexier' cousin 'practice'. But it is a mistake to think of theory and practice as opposites. Theory, when done well, is a practical activity. It is the process of forming new ideas, creating new knowledge and changing how we think about the world.

Activity 2.1

Any person educated within a large system will feel supported by, and alienated by, that system at different times.

Think about your own educational history. Tell a story to another student about a time when you felt like you did not fit into the educational system you were in – a moment when you felt like you were not cut out for learning. Then hear your partner's narrative. As you listen, think of a single word to describe the experience and how they felt. Then look in a thesaurus and find an unfamiliar word that means the same thing – the kind of word that you might expect to read in an academic text book but not use in everyday conversation with your friends. Put your name and the year in brackets after this word and you have the beginnings of a theory that can be used to discuss and explore ideas about ways in which education excludes and discomforts members of society in various ways. Now you are becoming an academic, as this is how academic work typically happens – often we need an unfamiliar word to describe a common experience as this distances us from the everyday and allows us time and space for 'doing theory' on it.

The idea of theory

For the reasons we have begun to outline, the need to theorize educational work is of considerable importance. One of the common challenges that confront students new to the study of education is the need to *interrogate* and *substantiate* their experiences, observations, ideas, claims and aspirations in the field of education. It is not surprising then that at first they find this difficult to do, for, like so many of the issues relating to education, 'theory' is also one of those labels that is more complicated than it at first might seem.

A useful account of the idea of theory can be found in Wellington's (2004) discussion of theory in educational research. Originating from the ancient Greek *theor* this involves the notion of the spectator or envoy – a person engaged in a *practical* and *critical* activity.

By around the seventeenth century, however, an unhelpful distinction between theory and practice began to emerge, with theory being regarded as a mental activity divorced from the practice of the field: 'the speculative and the practical' (Williams, 1983: 316), 'that's all very well in theory but how will it work in practice?'

For writers Carr and Kemmis (1986) the idea of *praxis* (another concept rooted in Greek philosophy) predates this *separation* of theory and practical knowledge, and, more usefully, *connects* theory and practice through a *dialectical* approach to thinking. *Dialectical* thinking is important in our study of education as it involves searching out contradictions that exist in particular educational issues through *reflection* on the many contributing elements. It is a process where *informed action* is actively re-shaped through the continuous review of the actions and the knowledge which inform it.

Theories, of the practical sort are used to explain why or how events, patterns, experiences and so on might appear as they do. Theorizing education involves students in *observing, listening, sensing, reflecting upon, reading* (in both senses of the word), *researching* and *questioning our interpretations* of particular educational phenomena (although this may not necessarily happen in that order). Importantly, such explanations are human by design and are, therefore, open to question, improvement and rejection. Theorizing is therefore always *provisional* – and the academic language of observation, interrogation and reporting should reflect this.

Here are two pieces of writing, both on the same topic – recent changes to education in England – by Education Studies undergraduates.

Case Study 2.1

Extract 1:

I would argue that over the past twenty years we have witnessed a relentless series of market orientated reforms which have further distorted principles of equality and moral purpose in education. As Porter observed in 1999 'education has become narrowed to an economic function . . . governments are effectively neutralizing schools, colleges and universities as independent and democratic institutions' (Porter, 1999: 11). This preoccupation with marketization can in fact be linked to a wider concern regarding Britain's continued competitiveness within a global market economy. In order to maintain the competitive nature of the UK economy, the government appears to be encouraging competition in a deliberate effort to prepare its citizens for the rigours of a global jobs market. Yet again we are faced with an apparent conflict between what Gamble (1994) describes as 'a liberal tendency which argues the case for a freer, more open, and more competitive economy, and a conservative tendency which is more interested in restoring social and political authority throughout society'.

⇨

> **Case Study 2.1—cont'd**
>
> **Extract 2:**
>
> The National Curriculum has increased standards and ensured consistency in schools. In addition, parents now have more information about the quality of teaching and achievement rates in schools, which previously only the middle classes could access. In my work placement I assisted a teacher in a year 9 English class and it was clear that, by referencing national curriculum criteria she was able to plan lessons with confidence that the teaching would be at the right level and cover the same material as other schools. On the other hand some teachers and academics argue that this approach stifles creativity.

At first glance these two extracts might not seem so different. After all, both deal with an aspect of educational policy, both present contrasting arguments or ideas and the first goes further by linking the personal, 'practical' experience of work placement to the abstract, 'theoretical' essay. But as we will demonstrate in this chapter, the first extract *theorizes* education. The second tries to, but does not manage it. There are no references to writing, policy or research – who are the people that argue about the stifling of creativity? There are three unsubstantiated, unsupported and 'taken for granted' assertions – for example, what are standards, what is consistency, and what is the evidence that only middle-class parents had access (and what does 'middle class' actually mean)? The first extract interrogates education as a social practice and it makes clear connections to broader social, economic and political factors. Most importantly, it makes very clear that what is presented here is argument rather than fact and it references two academic sources – Porter and Gamble.

Being theoretical

Being theoretical, in an active, engaged way, is different to simply learning theory that other people have come up with and writing about it. Education Studies draw together ideas from a range of existing academic disciplines – typically, these include Psychology (how people learn, how individuals function mentally, how a person's identity is formed and how this informs their educational experiences), Sociology (how education functions within broader social structures and the degree of agency individuals have within this), Cultural Studies (how education relates to peoples' other cultural experiences), Philosophy (what education is, its purpose and goals within a range of complex ideas about truth, values, humanity and morality) and the History of Education. Here we will consider one example of each, and demonstrate how using these academic approaches to *be* theoretical differs from simply 'passing on' the existing material.

Working with Psychology: Example 1 – assessment

During an Education Studies course, students will certainly come across theories about how people learn, and perhaps more importantly, how they do not – what stops them. In schools, both in the United Kingdom and abroad, the theories of Howard Gardner (1993) have become highly popular. In particular, his theory of multiple intelligences has been simplified and applied in the form of 'learning styles' – with students being categorized as visual, auditory or kinaesthetic learners. Gardner's theory of multiple intelligences is related to psychological ideas about how the mind functions and it is interesting because Gardner moves us away from thinking of intelligence as a fixed, stable category (such as IQ) and helps us to imagine intelligence as fluid, varied and individual. So we might think of David Beckham ordinarily as lacking intelligence, but Gardner's theories enable us to think of him as highly intelligent kinaesthetically but limited in terms of oral articulation – these are different forms of intelligence. But because students are doing Education Studies and not Psychology, the job at this point is not to simply 'learn Gardner' but to put his ideas into dialogue with other theoretical ideas about education. One example is assessment. If Gardner has helped us realize that there are lots of different forms of intelligence, then why does our educational system always privilege a very narrow range of these, often tested in artificial, stressful conditions such as examinations? We will find that the reasons are to do with the role of education in the broader social structure and the need for it to function as a mechanism for ranking people and equipping them (or not) with cultural capital (qualifications) that they can exchange for salaries and recognition. At this point the psychological ideas about the mind come into dialogue with sociological, philosophical and cultural ideas about what education is actually *for*.

Working with Sociology: Example 2 – cultural capital

So if assessment is geared towards one form of intelligence and the outcome is that only a minority of people get high enough grades to progress, then we may come to the conclusion that the exchange of cultural capital is unfair. Cultural capital is a sociological term associated with (Bourdieu and Passeron, 1990). His idea was that there are two forms of capital – money (economic capital) and cultural capital. The latter is the range of things you can collect and exchange that give you 'distinction' from other people. You cannot directly buy them but you are more likely to acquire them if you have money. These are qualifications from respected institutions, clothes, property and other symbols of status. The complex thing is this – it is possible to be poor but to have cultural capital. You might be an Oxford graduate who has never had a job, for example. So education serves to provide people with more or less cultural capital, and in England at least, a degree from one University is 'worth' more than the same degree from another. This relates to philosophical ideas about the nature of education.

Working with Philosophy: Example 3 – Plato and Mill

Two philosophers with greatly contrasting ideas about education were Plato and John Stuart Mill. Plato (1988) believed that society was best organized by dividing people into three groups. The rulers (the aristocracy) were simply a superior race of people than the workers who were essentially slaves. But their power was reliant on the work of another group, the

Guardians, who keep order and ensure the efficient administration of the society. This tripartite model can be found in the class system, some would argue – upper, middle and lower class people. John Stuart Mill's (1986) philosophy of education is described as 'utilitarianism' – everything should be done for the good of the highest number of people, and education empowers people and is good for them, thus education should be free for all and equal for all. This is the comprehensive view of education. But in England, we might find that, despite appearances, our school system, college structure and University provision resembles Plato's ideas more clearly. Private schools, grammar schools, comprehensive schools, specialist status schools and academies offer different 'types' of people different forms of education. So we end up realizing that what might seem like abstract philosophies actually resonate loudly with social practices. And we can easily relate the psychological ideas about how different people learn to some of Plato's ideas about differences between types of people and what education each group should have.

Working with Cultural Studies: Example 4 – technology and the 'Disconnect'

David Buckingham (2007) suggests that some young people today are so immersed in a culture of media, social networking and online creativity that they feel a profound disconnection from the technically barren world of school. He argues that the web 2.0 experiences of children demand a response from education and that ignoring the range of literacy practices students are engaged in out of school is dangerous. Opinion is divided over this. Some educators see videogames, media, mobile technologies and the internet as a problem – an obstacle to literacy. Others, like Buckingham, see the potential for schools to 'reach out' to the kinds of creative, communication experiences that new technologies have afforded, and most importantly, they see these as learning experiences. James Paul Gee (2003) suggests that playing a videogame is actually a literacy practice in itself. These are pertinent issues for the student of education, but like the other theoretical ideas we have discussed, just knowing what Buckingham thinks will not get one very far in Education Studies. Students need instead to put his thoughts into dialogue with sociological ideas about education and the 'insulation' between school and students' cultural experiences outside of the classroom. And it is important to consider these notions that new technologies offer rich cognitive experiences by putting them in touch with psychological theories about learning and intelligence. In addition, students might purposely engage with 'postmodern' philosophies about digital culture, virtual experiences and the challenged nature of reality, and what education might do in response to all this change.

Working with the History of Education: Example 5 – The 1988 National Curriculum

The history of education, offers another 'lens' through which we can examine education as a phenomenon which is situated in time and space. For many people the idea of a National

Curriculum is a way of ensuring equality of provision – with all children and pupils getting the same curriculum diet wherever they happen to go to school. Some believe that society needed a National Curriculum because before 1988 schools just 'did there own thing' and it was time for change.

Placing the idea of a National Curriculum 'in dialogue' invites us to evaluate some of these common assumptions. The History of Education reveals that educational interventions on this scale are more often than not related to economic imperatives of the time, such as economic recession, workforce reform, changes in the global labour market and so on. The processes of design and 'delivery' of the curriculum also says something about the extent of political control being exercised at the time. For example, commentators at the time were quick to note the remarkable similarity between the 1988 National Curriculum and the 1904 Board of Education Codes (Aldrich, 1988). In 'dialoguing' with history of education we locate educational policy and practices within a historical and cultural continuum.

Theoretical remixing

These brief examples serve to demonstrate the way Education Studies student needs to do theory, which is very different to the student of Sociology, Cultural Studies, Philosophy, Psychology or History. A theoretical idea about education needs to be understood, applied but then tested out in relation to ideas from the other disciplines and in relation to the lived experiences of the people involved in education – teachers, students, parents, employers, government and those excluded from or disengaged by education. And there must be a reflective dialogue between these theoretical ideas and students' own cultural situatedness – How are they constructed as a social subject, and what part has education played, and is it still playing, in this construction of identity? We might call this active engagement with and negotiation of theory as remixing it – reworking, exploring, creating ideas out of these theoretical stimuli. This 'remixing' is a way of thinking that is *dialectical*.

Interpretation and dialectical thinking

Interpreting educational phenomena and applying dialectical thinking is an important skill that we have to learn to practise in the study of education. A useful starting point for this is what C Wright Mills (1959) calls the 'Sociological Imagination'. The sociological imagination enables us to see the relationship of our personal biography to the wider events of society at large. This involves us by not simply taking things as given, or at first sight, but requires us to consider 'alternative futures' or possibilities. In applying the sociological imagination we come to consider a particular event or occurrence from a variety of angles or standpoints – as if looking through different 'lenses' which are then placed into the kind of dialogues we have outlined above. In doing so it enables us to consider alternative possibilities.

Activity 2.2

Choose one of the following for discussion:

1. Why is it that standards in state education are in decline?
2. How do children with Attention Deficit Hyperactivity Disorder experience life in school?
3. What is the connection between healthy eating and improvement in the educational performance of fourteen-year olds?
4. Should we encourage the continuance of faith schools?
5. When should we start compulsory education and when should it end?

In applying the sociological imagination, here are some of the ways we might consider these question and their underlying dialogues.

1. What are educational standards? In what ways can they be defined – if at all? Who decides what constitutes education standards? Who does this involve? Do standards change? Do they matter? If so, to whom? What would you consider to be your own educational standards, are they the same as your friends'?
2. What is an attention deficit? What makes a disorder a disorder? Who decides? Who does it affect? What does it mean for the people who are deemed to have it? What might it mean for carers, parents, teachers, governors? What does it mean for those deemed not to have it?
3. How do we define healthy eating? Why should we control what children and adolescents eat in school? Who should control what children and adolescents eat in school? Is there any demonstrable educational benefit?
4. How are faith schools different to any other type of school? How do we know this? By what criteria are we judging their success or usefulness to society? What are the issues surrounding community, equality, access, spirituality, indoctrination and segregation?
5. Is early intervention in education a good or bad thing? What might educational intervention involve? Who benefits – parents, government, the economy, children? Should we raise the school leaving age? What would the consequences be?

Each of these educational 'problems' requires that we first exercise something of the sociological imagination in order to consider them from a variety of angles. To do this we first have to begin to recognize and then suspend our predispositions and biases that may cloud our 'reading' and interpretation of the issue – this is not always easy to do when we are likely to have a vested interest in a particular stance related to the issue or unique positive or negative experiences. It may be something that is deeply embedded in our cultural experience and expectations that make it difficult to stand apart from. It is here that out ability to theorize becomes important through combining the skills of critical interpretation with an increasing knowledge of the field of study in the ways that we have previously described.

Strengthening the 'remix': Developing a praxis of critical judgement

From the starting point of 'thinking out' educational issues through using the sociological imagination and dialectical thinking, students will quickly realize that the former becomes increasingly superficial and the latter increasingly difficult without a supporting 'scaffold' of educational concepts to *inform* this theorizing. So it is essential that students get into some good practices of studentship early in their study of education:

Example of Good Practice

1. **Get inquisitive**. Ask yourself questions and examine and challenge your own ideas and convictions.
2. **Develop a reading strategy.** Target your reading to encompass chapters from essential and recommended texts, journal articles, broadsheets, reliable websites and so on. Familiarize yourself with 'field' through sampling the literature, begin to recognize some of the competing arguments, interests, 'contenders' and biases.
3. **Evaluate your position.** Ask yourself where you stand on the issue in question – if you do not know or do not care, then you have some work to do! Get inquisitive!
4. **Keep a reflective journal.** A reflective journal (hardcopy or electronic) in which to record your evolving perceptions, thoughts, arguments around what you have read, discussed, observed and heard – make it at a habit.
5. **Learn to embrace ambiguity.** Education and its processes rarely work in 'straight lines'. Be ready for discomfort, confusion and the occasional headache. You will, out of necessity, be frequently working in the 'grey areas' of educational thinking.
6. **'Dialogue' educational issues** and 'problems' with informing disciplines (see p.__).
7. **Rehearse your arguments and get critical.** Think through your lines of inquiry and argument. Finding time to do this may not always be easy, but is an extremely important part of the 'doing theory' process. Look for structure and pattern in your thinking, evaluate the arguments.
8. **Commit your thinking in writing – frequently.** Practise, practise and practise – draft and redraft your work – aim to ensure clarity and critical quality (this is a skill to be developed).
9. **Review your work.** Tutors will have something to say about your work, recommendations to offer, criticisms to make and, occasionally, praise to heap – review your work in light of this.
10. **Be collaborative be independent.** 'Doing Theory' in Educational Studies involves our ability to undertake solitary reflective work and collaborative discursive work – be prepared to do both in equal measure.

And remember – 'There is nothing so practical as a good theory' (Lewin, 1946: 169 quoted in Wellington, 2004: 25).

Summary

- the idea of what is theory has been discussed
- examples of 'being theoretical' have been explored
- good practice in 'remixing' theory has been addressed

References

Aldrich, R (1988) 'The National Curriculum: an historical perspective', in Lawton, D and Chitty, C (eds), *The National Curriculum*. London: Institute of Education

Bourdieu, P and Passeron, J (1990) *Reproduction in Education, Society and Culture*. London: Sage

Buckingham, D (2007) *Beyond Technology: Children's Learning in the Age of Digital Culture*. London: Polity

Carr, W and Kemmis, S (1986) *Becoming Critical: Education, Knowledge and Action Research*. London: Falmer Press

Gamble, A (1994) *The Free Economy and the Strong State: The politics of Thatcherism*. London: Macmillan

Gardner, H (1993) *Multiple Intelligences: The Theory in Practice*. New York: Basic Books

Gee, J P (2003) *What Video Games Have To Teach Us about Learning and Literacy*. New York: Palgrave MacMillan

Lewin, K (1946) 'Action research and minority problems', *Journal of Social Issues*, 2(34–6), 286 quoted in Wellington, J (2004) *Educational Research: Contemporary Issues and Practical Approaches*. London: Continuum

Mill, J S (1986) *Utlilitarianism*. London: Fontana Press

Plato (1988) *The Republic*. London: Penguin

Porter, J (1999) *Reschooling and the Global Economic Future*. Wallingford: Symposium

Wellington, J (2004) *Educational Research: Contemporary Issues and Practical Approaches*. London: Continuum

Williams, R (1983) *Key Words: A Vocabulary of Culture and Society*. London: Fontana Press

Wright Mills, C (1959) *The Sociological Imagination*. Oxford: Oxford University Press

Further reading

Carr, D (2003) *Making Sense of Education: An Introduction to the Philosophy and Theory of Education and Teaching*. London: RoutledgeFalmer

Hayes, D (2004) (ed.) *The RoutledgeFalmer Guide to Key Debates in Education*. London: RoutledgeFalmer

Useful websites

www.athens.ac.uk/ – The Athens electronic journal access website, which you will be able to register with through your University or College. Ask the staff in your library. Keeping up to date with journal articles is even more important than reading recommended books.

www.login.hope.ac.uk/ – The British Education Studies Association, a subject group for academics, researchers and students, who host an annual conference and publish a journal.

www.ioewebserver.ioe.ac.uk/ioe/cms/get.asp?cid=2772 – The Institute of Education's research website. Use this site to access information about research projects the Institute is conducting.

www.news.bbc.co.uk/1/hi/education/default.stm – BBC News Education site – essential for keeping up to date with educational policy, news and the public debates around education and schools.

www.education.guardian.co.uk/ – Education Guardian website – complements the above BBC site very well.

www.en.wikipedia.org/wiki/Education – Wikipedia's starting point for education. Not all academics value this kind of web 2/0 information source, so be careful. We advise you NOT to quote or reference Wikipedia, but to use it as a source through which you can access academic material. It offers an excellent 'gateway' to a host of perspectives on education and the broad range of references to books and journal articles are most useful.

www.tlrp.org/ – Teaching and Learning research programme website. Provides information on a range of research projects aimed at improving outcomes for learners in a range of contexts.

www.newman.ac.uk/subject_areas/Education/?pg=752 – Websites produced by third-year Education Studies undergraduates at Newman University College. The web links and journal reviews will be useful in relation to a range
of topic areas.

Useful search terms

education

theory

praxis

cultural capital

sociology of education

psychology of education

history of education

Comparative Education

Brendan Bartram

Introduction

The nature of comparative education is dealt with in this chapter. This particular area of educational enquiry rests on a long tradition, and the chapter outlines its early origins and the ways in which the discipline has evolved. In the process, it explores its various aims and purposes, and the reasons why in recent years international educational comparisons have become the focus of growing attention around the world, not least of all in political circles. Finally, the chapter considers a number of important pitfalls and dangers that can be associated with activity in this field – problems that need to be firmly borne in mind if comparative studies are to produce valid and meaningful data.

What is comparative education?

The study of education uses a range of critical lenses through which to view and explore the nature of educational processes. Some of these lenses are explicitly sociological, psychological, historical or political, and they are frequently combined to provide a sharply focused analysis of educational issues. In one sense, comparative education is simply an additional lens that can be applied to deepen our understanding of the nature of schools and schooling, and as such, it joins ranks with the other fields identified above that seek to make sense of these internal educational workings. However, given its potential to offer sophisticated insights into these processes by virtue of its ability to integrate multiple theoretical perspectives and contexts, comparative education is an important field of study in its own right, and this is reflected in its long history as an educational discipline.

The origins of the discipline are often associated with a number of nineteenth century personalities such as the Frenchman Victor Cousin, the German Friedrich Thiersch, Mathew Arnold in England and Horace Mann in the United States.

Further Reading

Victor Cousin (1772–1867) was responsible for major primary education reforms in France in the 1830s. His ideas were largely derived from his experiences of the school system in the German state of Prussia. Subsequently, he travelled to a number of other countries and published influential reports recommending educational change in his home country.

Friedrich Thiersch (1784–1860) made a number of visits to The Netherlands, Belgium and France where he collected copies of government reports on education, statistics, curricula, timetables and so on for analysis and consulted a range of educational experts. His experiences were important in influencing developments in the southern German state of Bavaria where he was a leading educationist in the 1830s.

Mathew Arnold (1822–1888), a leading educational inspector in England, made several visits to schools in France, Switzerland, Germany and The Netherlands as part of a fact-finding mission for the Newcastle Commission (1861) and the Taunton Commission (1868), whose findings were to have a particular steer on elementary and secondary school reforms in England.

In the United States, Horace Mann was instrumental in promoting educational democratization, based on his travels to countries such as Ireland, Scotland, Germany and France, an idea which he passionately defended in official reports in his capacity as secretary of the Massachusetts Board of Education. On his visits to German schools in Prussia, he was particularly impressed by the absence of corporal punishment, and drew repeatedly on his experiences here to support his vision of a more humane and democratic vision of education in the United States.

You may wish to look further into the work of the above figures – search the internet for details of their work in education and their main achievements.

These educationists, 'motivated by a desire to gain useful lessons from abroad' (Noah and Eckstein, 1969: 15) were among the first to produce reports examining and comparing aspects of education in other countries. Many of these reports had an influence on educational developments in the authors' home countries. Such early government-driven interest in foreign systems of education has continued and indeed expanded since these times, and has been accompanied by an increase in the numbers of scholars, researchers and universities around the world interested in establishing and describing the nature and parameters of comparative education as a discipline, the research methodologies that underpin it, and the ways in which it usefully contributes to our understanding of education.

The result of this growth is a diverse, multidisciplinary field of international educational enquiry. As such, comparative education accommodates many different areas of interest and styles of investigation. Some scholars and studies are more concerned with defining the nature of the discipline, the processes of policy borrowing (Phillips and Ochs, 2004), and the merits and demerits of the research approaches made use of. Large-scale comparative studies (e.g. the Trends in International Mathematics and Science Study [TIMSS] and Programme for International Student Assessment [PISA] surveys) often address a range of educational indicators across the world (learner participation and attainment, educational funding). Some studies focus on broader theoretical issues, relating for example to the ways in which social and political ideologies impact on educational systems and filter down to individual schools, teachers and learners (Holmes and McLean, 1989). Others examine and compare whole systems of education (the systems approach) or indeed very particular themes and issues in multiple settings (the themes approach) – the nature of pupil attitudes to particular school subjects; issues in primary education (Alexander, 2001); the organization and development of school curricula/adult education/vocational education; funding and management mechanisms; the construction of learner identities; teaching, learning and assessment strategies and so on. Much of the work that is carried out under the banner of comparative education is prompted by different aims and subject to a range of potential pitfalls, and these diverse goals and problems form the focus of the following sections.

Further Reading

You can find out more about the PISA and TIMMS educational surveys and results by visiting the following websites:

www.pisa/oecd.org
www.iea.nl/timms2007.html

Activity 3.1

Choose two education systems and produce an analytical comparison using the headings in the following box as a framework to structure your comparison of both systems. Eurydice has an excellent database of all European education systems – go to www.eurdice.org and click on the Eurybase link.

A) social and political contexts
B) underlying principles/ideologies
C) broad goals
D) structure of system
E) content – subjects and curriculum
F) teaching and learning principles
G) assessment – formats and frequency
H) key issues/developments

Why compare? The aims of comparative education

There are of course many reasons for making educational comparisons. One justification is simply that 'comparing is a fundamental part of the thought processes which enable us to make sense of the world' (Phillips, 1999: 15). Alexander (1999: 27) goes on to suggest that 'comparison is actually essential to educational progress . . . education by its nature requires hard choices of both a technical and moral kind. To make such choices requires an awareness of options and alternatives, together with the capacity to judge what is most fitting.' These points of view touch on two ideas that are central to comparative education – the notions of understanding and progress/improvement. Though the appeal of the 'improvement motive' has significantly served to raise the comparative profile in recent years, the idea that we can refine our understanding and knowledge through comparing is an equally valid reason for examining other systems and aspects of education. As Lauwerys and Tayar (1973: xii) explain:

> Comparative education is not, in essence, normative: it does not prescribe rules for the good conduct of schools and teaching. It does not aim at laying down what should be done. It does not offer views as to what education ought to be like. It attempts only to understand what is being done and why.

Understanding any aspect of education always requires an equally developed understanding of the social context in which it is rooted. How would a Japanese researcher make sense of the Sure Start educational initiative in Britain, for example, without an understanding of the social issues and problems that lay behind its introduction? This important connection between society and education is something that has long united all comparativists, and the words of Michael Sadler are often quoted in this respect:

'In studying foreign systems of education we should not forget that the things outside the school matter even more than the things inside the schools, and govern and interpret the things inside.'(Sadler in Higginson, 1979: 49)

Understanding how society influences education is thus a central concern for comparativists, though it presents them with a rather difficult challenge. Cowen (2005: 179) explains why this is the case:

> How do societies relate to (that is, affect, shape, influence, frame, penetrate or determine) educational systems and their components, such as teacher education provision, types of schools, administrative structures, universities, examination systems and so on? The problem is a tricky one because clearly, history, economics, social stratification patterns, politics and religious belief systems are all potentially forces that define the 'nature' of societies, and in ways that are not crystal clear, extend into the institutional patterns of educational systems . . . and curriculum practices.

The work of Holmes and McLean (1989) on educational ideologies represents an important contribution to our understanding of this relationship. The authors draw on the notion of ideology in an attempt to explain how prevalent beliefs and values in different societies have steered educational developments in particular directions. Their analysis contrasts the ideologies of essentialism, encyclopaedism and pragmatism, and provides us with a set of explanatory strategies for understanding and evaluating linkages between education and society. Within their discussion of essentialism, the authors describe a hierarchical, non-utilitarian and elitist view of education based on Platonic principles which sees clear divisions between vocational and academic education. They connect this philosophy to the English classical humanist ideology and elaborate on the notions of morality, specialization and individuality which they argue to be central influences on the English educational tradition.

This is compared with encyclopaedism, an ideology associated with the Czech philosopher Comenius, and regarded as having been particularly influential in many Continental European countries. Holmes and McLean describe this philosophy as being 'based on the premise that the content of education should include all human knowledge' (1989: 11), and they go on to discuss how this idea became especially influential in post-revolutionary France, where the notions of rationality, universality and utility that underpin the encyclopaedic vision of education were embraced because of their democratizing potential. The authors discuss how the influence of this view spread across many parts of Europe, to countries as geographically diverse as Spain and Russia (though England remained untouched!), despite a number of differences in interpretations and emphases.

Pragmatism is another ideology examined by the authors, this time ascribed to the influence of the American educationalist Dewey. They discuss a naturalistic view of education that concentrates on learner needs, social interaction and the relationship between the individual and society, and defines education chiefly in terms of social processes and personal development. The distinction between education and training so pronounced within the essentialist view described above is considered to be an artificial and unhelpful division within this view of education.

Activity 3.2

Search the internet for information on classical humanism, encyclopaedism and pragmatism/naturalism. Birgit Pepin's article 'Curriculum, Cultural Traditions and Pedagogy' is a useful starting point, and is available at: www.leeds.ac.uk/educol.documents/000000872.htm. When you have made notes, consider the following question and statements:

- In what ways do the ideological principles described above translate into educational practices in countries with which you are familiar? Consider possible connections between these ideas and the structure of education systems, the nature and content of the curriculum, the relationship between academic and vocational education, approaches to teaching and learning, pupil organization (mixed ability and setting, streaming, differentiation), prevalent forms of assessment and so on.
- research and discuss some of the key differences between education systems that have been strongly influenced by encyclopaedic traditions (e.g. the Danish and French systems, the German and Japanese systems).
- compare and contrast the key features of classical humanism and encyclopaedism, and encyclopaedism and pragmatism.

Is there any room to argue that recent trends and developments in English education are moving us away from our classical humanist ideological roots? What evidence, if any, can you find to support these arguments?

Examining the ways in which ideologies can provide us with tools for understanding the relationship between education systems and societies is clearly useful to a degree, though some would suggest that more sophisticated tools are required, and that the above ideologies limit us to explaining education in largely euro-centric terms, notwithstanding the extent to which many non-European systems have been influenced by European models of education through policy borrowing or as a result of colonialism. Understanding the socio-educational connection is, however, only one aim of comparative education, and the following section will now look more broadly at the other goals attributed to the endeavour.

Additional aims

As suggested above, one of the key motivations of many scholars in the field is the quest for educational improvement in terms of policy and practice. Though this is not necessarily as straightforward a process as some might believe, learning from elsewhere is a laudable goal with many potential benefits. In one respect, examining other education systems can guard against educational complacency and stagnation at home, since the process of comparing can engender a questioning attitude that highlights the potential of alternative ways of doing things. This can lead to a re-evaluation of current practices, and identify new possibilities and departures. Phillips (2000), for example, discusses how long-standing British interests in the German education system have been implicated in a number of developments in England from the establishment of a national system of education in the nineteenth century, to the way in which German approaches to curriculum and assessment were used to inform the debate leading up to the Education Reform Act in 1988.

Investigating other systems and achieving a greater understanding of the ways in which social contexts variously influence education can also go some way towards fostering 'cooperation and mutual understanding among nations by discussing cultural differences and similarities and offering explanations for them' (Phillips, 2000: 298). Though this might be considered a rather abstract aim, more immediate applications can be identified in terms of both positive and negative 'learnings'. Many European universities have, for example, restructured their courses around semester and credit systems based on perceived organizational advantages offered by the American model, while comprehensivization in England in the 1960s attracted a great deal of attention around the world from countries interested in moving away from selective forms of secondary education. Looking elsewhere can also alert educationists, and indeed policy-makers, to potential pitfalls, though such lessons are not always heeded. In this respect, the problems encountered in relation to American vocational reforms in the 1980s come to mind – if heeded more fully, some of the initial and more persistent difficulties that surrounded the introduction of National Vocational Qualifications in England could arguably have been removed. In this way, comparative education can act as a kind of educational laboratory, highlighting the effects of particular variables and the results of a range of 'experiments' in different parts of the world, though interpreting these lessons is often somewhat problematic.

Comparative education can also render a useful service in terms of identifying factors which appear to be of universal importance in education, and those which are more context dependent. Osborn et al. (2003) refer to this discussion in terms of 'constants' and 'contexts', and their work examining pupils' attitudes to school life and learning in England, France and Denmark offers an interesting illustration of this dual categorization. Among the factors that emerged as important irrespective of national context, the authors identified a strong belief by pupils in the connection between education and their economic futures, the importance of interactive and enjoyable lesson activities, concerns about the impact of assessment, and the significance of respect between pupils, peers and teachers. As such, the authors are able to suggest that the degree of commonality here supports the wider relevance of these findings, whereas other results indicate that the importance of certain other factors is more contingent on context. There were notable differences, for example, in the pupils' definitions of successful teacher–pupil relationships, in the way they conceived of home–school connections, and the ways in which they constructed their identities as learners within the school and classroom contexts.

Current interest in comparative education

As is by now clear, interest in comparative education is not new; though this interest has arguably intensified in recent decades for a number of reasons. Some of these relate to the greater ease with which it is now possible to experience other education systems. The rise in the number of exchange and mobility programmes means that students and staff have become increasingly involved in many forms of international educational collaboration, and this first-hand experience is often the motive for deeper exploration of similarities and differences between systems. Other developments in travel, media, the advent of the internet and Information and Communications Technology (ICT), and changes in geopolitical relations have added to these impetuses to look beyond borders in all spheres of life, including education. Accompanying demands for greater transparency and comparability of qualifications by an increasingly mobile 'global' workforce have led to further interest in the way in which education operates elsewhere. The biggest factor responsible for this growth in interest, however, is largely political, and centres around two related motives: economic competition and cost-effectiveness.

First, many commentators have referred to a growing educational instrumentalism – particularly in countries such as the United Kingdom and the United States – that has been driven by political beliefs in global economic interdependence and the role played by education in providing a national competitive edge in the new 'knowledge economy'. This belief, though very open to question, is a central feature of neo-liberal ways of thinking about education, and has increasingly led governments and policy-makers to examine what is happening in other education systems, especially in economically successful countries, in an attempt to consider what elements might be borrowed in order to boost economic health at home. Phillips and Ochs (2004: 778) discuss how these political motivations may prompt the 'internal dissatisfaction' that leads to such cross-national attraction, while Alexander (2001: 2) captures the essence of this kind of political thinking: 'The way to make good national economic deficiencies was to borrow the educational policies of a country's more successful economic competitors.'

This politically charged growth in interest has 'for the wider general public its most visible manifestation in . . . the shape of cross-national studies of educational achievement, and the widespread influence of related league tables' (Crossley, 2006: 7). The growing popularity of such international league tables has both promoted political interest in comparative education and increased political sensitivity to national rankings, to the extent that politicians may gear policy priorities towards improving perceived educational shortcomings on the one hand, and on the other, scrutinize practices from countries higher up the tables in a bid to identify (financially) efficient ways of addressing believed weaknesses. Though league tables can be informative in a number of ways, reliance on them as neutral and valid indicators brings with it a number of problems, and these issues will be examined more closely in the final section.

Activity 3.3

Search the internet to see what you can find out about the Organisation for Economic Cooperation and Development (OECD)-led Programme for International Student Assessment (PISA) study and the Trends in International Mathematics and Science Study (TIMSS). Consider and discuss the following issues:

Activity 3.3—cont'd

- Which countries appear to perform particularly well?
- What reasons (social and educational) *might* account for such performance?
- In what ways might it be dangerous to value any education system on the basis of its league position?

Finland and Korea are two countries which frequently perform very well in international league tables, and are both countries committed to comprehensive education – yet this system is often blamed for lower performance in the United Kingdom – how might we account for this?

Problems and dangers: The comparative minefield

Clearly, then, there is a great deal to be gained from comparisons in education, and a growing desire and interest to make them. However, what might seem a simple undertaking can often be dogged by a range of problems and dangers that call into question the very basis for making the comparisons in the first place. Perhaps the first issue here relates to validity – is the comparison being made a justifiable or valid one? This highlights perhaps the most important aspect of educational comparisons – the need to ensure, as far as possible, that 'like with like' is being compared, with any key contextual or background differences acknowledged so that the readers can judge for themselves the extent to which they feel the comparison is a valid one. As such, this need to compare like with like is one of the central tenets of the discipline (Grant, 1999: 132), and yet it is not always adhered to, or differences might not always be made sufficiently clear. Any comparison between secondary education in England and Germany, for example, would always be somewhat problematic, given fundamental differences in the way this sector is structured in both countries. In England, most pupils move from primary at 11 into comprehensive schools, where they will be taught with peers from across the ability range, most likely in different sets for particular subjects. This is highly unusual in Germany, which still operates a selective tripartite system. At age 11 or 12, German pupils move into one of three separate types of schools – a vocationally oriented school (Hauptschule), a general secondary modern equivalent (Realschule) and a grammar school (Gymnasium). Any comparison of pupil attainment between the two countries would clearly need to ensure that this difference had been taken into account – if the German sample was made up exclusively of Gymnasium pupils, then this would obviously distort the findings, given that the English comprehensive sample would represent a much wider range of ability. The lack of 'like for likeness' would clearly be unfair, and this would largely invalidate the comparison.

Such differences are of course common, and the particularities of each context will always require detailed discussion. For instance, comparisons between countries such as the United States, Canada, Australia, Germany and England or Japan are always somewhat difficult given the very different ways in which education is organized and managed. Education in Japan and England is similar in that both systems are centrally controlled, funded and directed, with national curricula dictated by the government. This is not the case in the other countries mentioned above, where the responsibility for education policy is devolved to the individual states, often resulting in quite different 'systems' within the same country, for example between Texas and New York in the United States, or Bavaria and North-Rhine-Westphalia in Germany.

Such differences are important and would need to be considered in a number of ways. One issue might, for example, relate to demographic differences in each setting that may again have important consequences for the validity of any comparison. One issue that is often raised with regard to comparisons of literacy levels between England and Japan, for example (which, as mentioned above, share a number of system similarities), concerns the background of pupils living in each country. Japan has a largely indigenous population, with very little immigration, and as such the overwhelming majority of Japanese pupils speak Japanese as their first language. This is rather different from the situation in England or France, both countries with sizeable linguistic minorities, and as such many pupils speak English or French as second languages. In comparative surveys of literacy, it is therefore unsurprising that Japanese pupils are often seen to 'outperform' French and English children. Ignoring such important contextual differences is therefore dangerous, since such detail is vital in allowing for a more accurate and informed interpretation of the data.

Even when such differences have been allowed for, it may still be necessary to scrutinize the educational contexts still further. Staying with the above theme, it will come as no surprise that literacy has been a key focus of the New Labour educational agenda in England (Alexander, 2001), and as such, comparisons often reveal that literacy levels in this country are ahead of a number of others. In a sense, this could be seen as unremarkable, given that improving literacy has been and continues to be a key educational aim in Britain. Such an aim, however, might not be quite so central elsewhere, and Murray Thomas (1990: 26) discusses how in different countries, very different goals may be emphasized within an education system – key aims may be the development of self-fulfilment, vocational skills, social cohesion and identity formation in the wake of political unrest and upheaval and so on. Comparisons may therefore sometimes simply reflect differences in political priorities and emphases, and it is important that they be interpreted in this light. It becomes dangerous, of course, when assumptions are made without bearing these contextual differences in mind.

Equivalence

A particular problem in comparative education relates to the issue of equivalence, linguistically and semantically. Comparing aspects of education elsewhere often means being confronted with different languages, where educational terms may carry different nuances or indeed have no exact equivalent. Grant (1999) discusses how the very word 'education' can be translated in very different ways in many languages, each with slightly different connotations. This applies equally to labels which many might consider unproblematic, such as primary education, though even this would be incorrect (primary school in England is generally from four to eleven, in Denmark it covers seven to sixteen!). Certain terms that we take for granted in English may have no exact equivalence in other languages or systems. The word 'accountability' has, for example, taken on a very particular meaning in English education since the 1988 Education Reform Act, given its associations with new forms of quality control and performance management. In many countries (such as France and Germany), these 'coatings' are absent, and the word is indistinguishable from the general word for responsibility. As such, cross-country studies examining teachers' understandings of accountability require careful thought and discussion if meaningful insights are to be produced.

Another example can be seen in the word 'private' when applied to education. In the English-speaking world, the use of this word is quite distinct from its use in Dutch education, where it is used to refer to state-funded schools that choose to develop their own curricula based on particular religious or philosophical principles. In the 1980s, Mrs Thatcher referred to the popularity and prevalence of Dutch 'private' schools in the Netherlands (around 75 per cent of Dutch schools fall within this category) on a number of occasions to support her argument for expanding private provision in England, without due regard for this very important conceptual distinction. This example again clearly highlights the need for careful consideration of background detail relating to the issues and countries being compared, and indeed the need to maintain a questioning attitude about the ways in which even apparently unproblematic terms may be used and understood in different settings.

Uncritical transfer

Many of the issues discussed above illustrate problems relating to validity, fairness and bias in educational comparisons. These problems can, however, become dangers if they are ignored or unexplored by politicians and policy-makers looking for quick-fix solutions or short-term political advantage. Crossley and Watson (2003: 39) discuss the dangers of cherry-picking particular successful practices from one country and applying them in another as 'education . . . cannot be decontextualised from its local culture'. Even though 'common problems may exist in different countries . . . solutions can rarely be found in the application of a common model across different cultures' (ibid.: 39). In this regard, Alexander (2001: 41) has been particularly critical of Labour's introduction of the literacy strategy in English primaries, based on observations in a number of countries: 'since the most striking pedagogical contrast was the much heavier use of whole class teaching in the classrooms of the Pacific Rim and Continental Europe, it was assumed that a shift to this method in English primary schools would make the desired difference, reverse years of national decline and simultan-eously propel Britain up the league tables'. In his view, introducing this strategy was based on the somewhat simplistic assumption that high levels of literacy in these countries related to this particular aspect of pedagogy. He argues that such an assumption 'enables governments to legitimate their claim that questions of quality in education can be resolved by attaching pedagogy while ignoring structure and resources'. (ibid.: 30)

Though many would support the success of the strategy, Alexander's point about solv-ing a multi-faceted problem by concentrating on one idea adopted from abroad remains a valid one, and many have argued that the strategy still works better in Japan, where trad-itional pedagogy dominates in the face of larger group sizes and greater cultural respect for teachers who face fewer discipline challenges. It should also be remembered that Japanese children's education is routinely supplemented by widespread use of crammer schools in the evenings, resulting in a great deal of extra education for most children, and accompanying improvements in academic achievement.

Many commentators are in fact highly critical of this kind of opportunistic borrow-ing, selective contextual scrutiny and 'uncritical international transfer' (Crossley, 2006: 11), motivated by political ends, especially where assumptions are made that borrowing success-ful practices from robust economies will bring equivalent economic success. As Robinson (1999: 223) argues, 'there is effectively no correlation between doing well in international tests . . . and overall economic performance,' and yet governments remain particularly sus-ceptible to these views. The growing popularity of international league tables is believed by many to exacerbate these pressures. Prais (2003) provides an excellent analysis of the vagaries of such international comparisons, discussing a range of bias and sampling issues that call into question the results of the recent PISA survey, from which England emerged particularly well with regard to mathematics, in contrast to an IEA survey conducted only one year previously. Issues of cultural bias are particularly relevant in such surveys too, with some suggestions that familiarity with test formats in certain countries (much has been made of a Japanese cultural bias towards exams, for example) may skew scores and there-fore not provide adequate representations of successful achievement. Inferring too much from such results is once again highly dangerous, and on this note, Alexander (2001: 2) offers a final cautionary reminder for all comparativists, but especially for those with pol-itical motivations: 'the cause–effect relationship between teaching strategies, educational league tables and national economic performance is far from proven'.

Conclusion

In conclusion, then, interest in comparative education seems unlikely to wane, given its potential to produce fresh insights into many aspects of education. As discussed, compara-tive studies have long covered a wide range of issues, and explored these from a number of theoretical angles. This diversity makes the field a particularly rich and dynamic one in terms of educational research. Some would suggest, however, that interest in achieving more detailed understandings of education has been fuelled in recent years by desires to learn lessons from abroad in the quest for economic and quick-fix improvement, as policy-makers increasingly incline towards a view of education as a key component in the economic race, against a backdrop of growing political sensitivities to international league table rankings. This situation calls for a heightened awareness of the many pitfalls, described above, which can severely compromise the value of any lessons learned from comparative studies – and highlights the importance of maintaining a critical attitude when studying education.

Activity 3.4

In groups, investigate an educational issue in four countries. This might be an aspect of the curriculum, a phase of education, an aspect of teaching, learning or assessment, a funding or management issue, a school subject, approaches to inclusion and so on.

You may find it useful to search national government websites, and visit Eurydice, the EU's education database (www.eurydice.org) and the World Education database (www.ibe.unesco.org).

Make a set of justified recommendations for educational change in one of the countries on the basis of practice in the other three, while acknowledging your awareness of the various constraints (cultural, social, political and so on) that might impede the successful implementation of your proposals for change. Present your findings to the wider group.

Summary

- comparative education is a long-established and diverse field of enquiry
- its aims include refining our understanding of education and identifying potential improvements
- comparative education attaches particular importance to the social context of educational issues
- comparisons should always highlight key contextual differences between countries if they aim to be valid and meaningful
- a range of factors pose threats to the validity of comparisons
- comparisons should clearly acknowledge what these factors are
- political and economic interests have recently fuelled a growth in educational comparisons and league tables
- the results of these league tables and comparisons require careful scrutiny and interpretation if erroneous conclusions are to be avoided

References

Alexander, R (1999) 'Culture in pedagogy, pedagogy across cultures', in Alexander, R, Broadfoot, P and Phillips, D (eds), *Learning from Comparing*. Oxford: Symposium Books

Alexander, R (2001) *Culture and Pedagogy*. Oxford: Blackwell

Cowen, R (2005) 'Extreme political systems, deductive rationalities and comparative education: education as politics', in Halpin, D and Walsh, P (eds), *Educational Commonplaces*. London: Institute of Education

Crossley, M (2006) Bridging Cultures and Traditions: Perspectives from Comparative and International Research in Education. A professorial address at the University of Bristol, 9 February 2006

Crossley, M and Watson, K (2003) *Comparative and International Research in Education.* London: RoutledgeFalmer

Grant (1999) 'Comparing educational systems', in Matheson, D and Grosvenor, I (eds), *An Introduction to Education Studies.* London: David Fulton

Holmes, B and McLean, M (1989) *The Curriculum: A Comparative Perspective.* London: Unwin Hyman

Lauwerys, J A and Tayar, G (1973) *Education at Home and Abroad.* London: Routledge and Kegan Paul

Murray Thomas, R (1990) *International Comparative Education.* Oxford: Butterworth-Heinemann

Noah, H J and Eckstein, M A (1969) *Towards a Science of Comparative Education.* London: Macmillan

Osborn, M, Broadfoot, P, McNess, E, Planel, C, Ravn, B and Triggs, P (2003) *A World of Difference? Comparing Learners Across Europe.* Maidenhead: OUP

Phillips, D (1999) 'On comparing', in Alexander, R, Broadfoot, P and Phillips, D (eds), *Learning from Comparing.* Oxford: Symposium Books

Phillips, D (2000) 'Learning from elsewhere in education: some perennial problems revisited with reference to British interest in Germany', *Comparative Education*, 36(3), 297–307

Phillips, D and Ochs, K (2004) 'Researching policy borrowing: some methodological challenges in comparative education', *British Educational Research Journal*, 30(6), 773–84

Prais, S (2003) 'Cautions on OECD's Recent Educational Survey (PISA)', *Oxford Review of Education*, 29, 2

Sadler, M (1900) 'How far can we learn anything of practical value from the study of foreign systems of education?' in Higginson, J A (1979) (ed.), *Selections from Michael Sadler: Studies in World Citizenship.* Liverpool: Dejall and Meyorre

Further reading

Alexander, R (2001) *Culture and Pedagogy.* Oxford: Blackwell

Alexander, R, Broadfoot, P and Phillips, D (ed.) (1999) *Learning from Comparing* Vol. 1, Oxford: Blackwell

Alexander, R, Osborn, M and Phillips, D (ed.) (2000) *Learning from Comparing* Vol. 2, Oxford: Blackwell

Armstrong, F and Barton, L (2000) *Inclusive Education: Policy, Contexts and Comparative Perspectives.* London: David Fulton

Brock, C and Tulasiewicz, W (2000) *Education in a Single Europe.* London: Routledge

Griffin, R (2001) *Education in Transition.* Oxford: Symposium

Mebrahtut, T, Crossley, M and Johnson, D (2000) *Globalisation, Educational Transformation and Societies in Transition.* Oxford: Symposium

Okano, K and Tsuchiya, M (1999) *Education in Contemporary Japan.* Cambridge: CUP

Phillips, D (ed.) (1995) *Aspects of Education and the European Union.* Oxford: Triangle Books

Poppleton, P, Menlo, A and Williamson, J (2004) *New Realities of Teachers' Work Lives.* Oxford: Symposium

Postlethwaite, N T (1996) *The International Encyclopaedia of National Systems of Education.* Oxford: Pergammon Press

Useful websites

www.baice.ac.uk – British Association for International and Comparative Education. Promotes research, activities and events in the field and produces *Compare*, a journal of comparative education.

www.eurydice.org – Eurydice – the information network on education in Europe. Gives access to information on education systems all over Europe, as well as produces reports on particular educational issues.

www.ibe.unesco.org – International Bureau of Education based in Geneva. Detailed reports are available on every education system in the world.

www.oecd.org – Organisation for Economic Cooperation and Development. Produces reports and analyses on a range of issues, including various aspects of education across the world.

www.pisa/oecd.org – Programme for International Student Assessment. The latest (and previous) surveys are available, along with details on how the surveys are carried out, participating countries and so on.

www.iea.nl/timms2007.html – Trends in International Mathematics and Science Study. Provides access to reports carried out in recent years, along with information on the surveys themselves.

Useful internet search terms

Japanese/French/Indian ministry of education, etc.

education in Germany/Scotland/Canada, etc.

international educational surveys

educational comparisons

maths teaching in Finland/Korea/Ireland, etc.

comparative education

schools in Russia/Peru/China, etc.

Ethics for Educators

Sue Warren and Susan Waltham

4

Chapter Outline

Education has notions such as "improvement," "betterment," and "the passing on of what is worth while" built into it. That education must involve something of ethical value is, therefore, a matter of logical necessity.

(Peters, 1966: 91)

Introduction and definitions

'Ethics' is a branch of the study of philosophy. In every day language, it is about 'right' and 'wrong' and can be confused with 'morals'. Ethics are considered to be overarching and globally applicable ideas. Morals can be regarded as the practical application of ethics, but there are problems with this simplistic definition. Morals are dependant on which nation, culture or religious group a person belongs to. They also change through time; think of the British Victorians who hid piano legs versus the wearing of bikinis on beaches by the modern British. 'Ethics' is not limited to specific acts and defined moral codes, but encompasses moral ideals and behaviours. A person's philosophy of life (personal ethics) is therefore a moral code applicable to an individual, while social ethics means moral theory applied to groups of people. Applied ethics is the application of ethical principles to particular real-life situations. Here in this chapter we look at ethics in education.

Definitions

The word 'ethics' comes from the Greek word '*ēthikē*' meaning character, nature or disposition. It can be said that a person is of 'good character' that is they are 'moral'. This means two distinct things. The first is that a person has an understanding of morals. In this meaning, the opposite is 'amoral' which means an inability to distinguish between right and wrong. The second meaning is that the person actively follows and practices the moral rules. This opposite of this is 'immoral', referring to actions that violate ethical principles. One important issue is how and when children and young people gain an understanding of morals, and whether this should be taught as part of an educational curriculum, another is how educators act in their everyday work with learners.

Historical background

To understand the contemporary position of ethics in education, a historical perspective is necessary. The western philosophical tradition began in ancient Greece in the sixth century BC. The first philosophers are called 'Pre-Socratic' meaning that they came before Socrates. Philosophy was first recorded as being applied to real life by Pythagoras (about 582–504 BCE) from whom it received its name which means 'the love of wisdom'. Pythagoras thought the world was dependent on number and in perfect harmony. He wanted humans to lead a 'harmonious life'. Socrates (469–399 BCE) was interested in the thoughts and opinions of people. He tried to define the virtues, such as courage and justice, by cross-examining people who professed to have knowledge of them.

Plato (428–348 BCE) incorporated ideas of earlier philosophers and developed a scheme with three aspects: dialectic, ethics and physics. He thought the three greatest virtues were Wisdom, Courage, and Temperance, and that these are united by virtue of Justice. The school founded by Plato, called the Academy continued for long after his death and supported the continued development of his ideas. The most important among Plato's disciples is Aristotle (384–322 BCE).

Philosophy to Aristotle meant science, and its aim was the recognition of the purpose in all things. Aristotle's followers continued to develop ideas, finally returning to the practical standpoint of Socratic ethics. Philosophical doctrines were popularized aiming to provide individuals with a fixed moral basis for life. This was seen as especially relevant in a time of general confusion and dissolution.

Immanuel Kant, an eighteenth-century German philosopher, followed this tradition. He is regarded as one of the most influential thinkers of modern Europe. He wrote of his philosophy and developed ethics as moral laws. During the nineteenth century, Thomas Percival, put ethical imperatives into codes, particularly for the medical profession. This established for the first time a set of rules for a particular profession.

> **Further Reading**
>
> Benn, P (1997) *Ethics*. London: Routledge (Fundamentals of Philosophy Series)
>
> Blackburn, S (2003) *Ethics: A Very Short Introduction*. Oxford: Oxford University Press
>
> Nagg, T (1987) *What Does it all Mean?* Oxford: Oxford University Press
>
> Tansio, T (2002) Understanding Ethics: An Introduction to Moral Theory. Edinburgh: Edinburgh University Press

The rise of modern ethical codes

The contemporary view of ethics is largely the result of radical changes in the global world view after World War II. For the first time, the ethics and moral codes of different cultures were compared and debated in the public realm. In 1949, the Nuremberg Military Tribunal that investigated war crimes including the holocaust, resulted in ten basic principles for ethical research on humans. Notable among them is the idea that individuals have to give their consent without force, deceit or coercion being used. This directly led to the development of medical ethics. In 1954, The World Medical Association published 'Principles for those in Research and Experimentation', which was then adopted in 1964 as the 'Declaration of Helsinki'. Also in 1964, the British Medical Research Association published 'Responsibility in Investigations on Human Subjects'. Medical ethical principles have been used as a basis for ethics within the field of sociology, psychology and education, particularly with regard to research.

> **Further Reading**
>
> These websites contain the individual associations' codes of ethical practice:
>
> www.bera.ac.uk – The British Educational Research Association
> www.bps.org – The British Psychological Association
> www.bsa – The British Sociological Association
> www.scre.ac.uk – The Scottish Council for Research in Education

Professional and global ethical codes of practice

Professional associations and institutions have their own ethical codes. Examples include the British Psychological Society and the British Sociological Association. For those professionals working in education, the British Educational Research Association, the National Education Association (NEA) in the United States and the General Teaching Council have ethical codes of conduct.

The United Nations Convention on the Rights of the Child (UNCRC) (UN, 1989) is an international human rights treaty that grants all children and young people (aged 17 and under) a comprehensive set of rights. The United Kingdom signed the convention on 19 April 1990, ratified it on 16 December 1991 and it came into force in the United Kingdom on 15 January 1992. The convention gives children and young people over 40 substantive rights. These include the right to access to services such as education and health care, special protection measures and assistance, grow up in an environment of happiness, love and understanding and develop their personalities, abilities and talents to the fullest potential.

The articles of the UNCRC are regarded as ethically sound by all those nations who have signed up to the convention. However, each nation has taken these articles and used them in their own cultural context. In the United Kingdom, legislation that effects children directly (such as statutory school starting age) and indirectly (such as family income support) is based upon British cultural values. This interpretation of the articles becomes increasingly problematic as the cultural diversity in British society increases. The position of faith schools (Christian, Jewish and Islamic), the contemporary debate about statutory school leaving age and the percentage of very young children in 'educare' are just three issues that have a resonance with the UNCRC stance. Legislation in the United Kingdom that refers directly to the UNCRC includes:

- The Children Act 1989 (HMSO, 1989)
- Protection of Children Act 1999 (HMSO, 1999)
- Every Child Matters (DfES, 2003)

Universities have Research Ethics policies and Research Ethics Committees, the Health Service has Local Research Ethics Committees (Department of Health, 1991), the role of these committees are to scrutinize research proposals and grant permission, or not, for the research to be carried out. Since the implementation of the *Every Child Matters* policy (DfES, 2003) inter-agency work is required to enable the required 'wrap around care' for children in schools, Extended Schools and Children's Centres. This move towards greater inter-professional collaboration has grown and at times the use of different codes of ethical practice may cause problems as several professional bodies may need to be approached for approval.

The Department for Education and Skills (DfES) set up the Teaching and Learning Research Project to actively encourage teachers to engage in classroom-based research, giving modest grants to those teachers. The approach which was advocated was Action Research, a particular process in which teachers and other practitioners research their own actions in the classroom in order to make improvements in their practice. Unfortunately, not all of these projects were really action research on practice and action in the classroom but became evaluations of schemes of work or focused on learning rather than the teaching which led to the learning. The premise upon which action research is based is that of collaboration and 'democratic and co-operative human relationships and contributions' and that the research is 'compatible with the educational aims of the situation under research' (Altrichter in Schratz, 1993: 44). In this form of research, the ethics are openly negotiated at the beginning and maybe several times during the process of the research. The ethical process is the responsibility of both the researcher and the participants leading to a sharing of power and status. This can be particularly problematic if the participants are children and the researcher is adult and their teacher.

Working with participants from different cultural backgrounds can cause problems for researchers and care must be taken to avoid misunderstandings. Barriers to understanding may exist which need to be considered carefully at the planning stage in order that unintentional disrespect is avoided. In some cultural groups, the community leader may need to be approached first as the power and responsibility lies at the community level rather than at the family or individual level. Language can be a barrier to full understanding between the research and the prospective participants. In some groups the written word may be the most acceptable way in which to gain informed consent, rather than a written reply. These difficulties are inter- and intra-national.

Childhood and the age of responsibility

'Childhood' is a concept that has changed and continues to change. The discussion of who is a 'child', and what marks the beginning and end of childhood, is a larger debate but has a bearing on the application of ethics within education (Cunningham, 2006; Hill and Tisdall, 1997).

Attitudes towards children (birth to 18) differ according to the age and their perceived role. The younger child is often seen as passive recipient of care, controllable; the older one as aggressive, or at least assertive, irresponsible trouble maker. This is reflected in a wide range of legislation and policy covering not just education but also health, social security, employment, housing and so on. Anomalies occur within this cultural perception of children, for example, those about children who care for a disabled relative, often their parent, and young people who are volunteers in their communities or ethical campaigners around ecological issues, anti-war and animal rights.

Activity 4.1 Age of Responsibility

How do we judge whether a child or young person understands the implications of his or her actions? What implications are there for ethical behaviour management strategies in schools? How do educational institutions deal with knife carrying, extremist political or religious views in ethical ways?

Activity 4.1 Age of Responsibility—cont'd

The Times Educational Supplement website www.tes.co.uk/ and www.education.guardian.co.uk/ The Guardian Unlimited Education website are both good places to start for contemporary and archived information on these issues. The children's commission also has a website that provides useful information: www.11million.org.uk/

Case Study 4.1

The 'citizenship agenda' in contemporary British politics is an area fraught with ethical issues. On the 5 March 2003, a large number of pupils left their schools in England and mounted a protest against the Iraqi war. Response to this protest was mixed. Some were arrested under public disorder act, others suspended or otherwise punished by their school. Some of the newspapers praised their action, others condemned it. Consider the views of the different participants in this event; the children and young people, their school teachers, their parents, the police, the politicians. A useful place to start is accessing the following article on the Guardian Unlimited website: Martin Wainwright, Thursday 6 March 2003 'Thousands of Pupils in Nationwide Protest', the *Guardian*.

What are the ethical issue here?

Ethical considerations when researching with learners, particularly children

As discussed above, professional ethical codes of practice and the law have differing views of the age at which children should be seen to be capable of making informed decisions. This also includes giving their consent to be engaged in research, either as a subject, or, more latterly, as a participant. Different codes for ethical research may set differing ages for such consent but most are clear that under the age stated, children should be asked for their *assent*, to agree for themselves whether or not to take part. How this is done, and at what age, varies accordingly. In medical research children may be engaged in trials of drugs or procedures. In these cases they are the subjects of research. Questions which must be asked in these cases are in the nature of how will the children, and others like them, benefit? Should the children know that they might be given a trial drug or a placebo? How will the control group be allowed access to procedures which prove to be efficacious for the experimental group once the research is over? These should all be answered before the research begins.

In certain child abuse situations it may be deemed more ethical for covert observations to be videoed and this evidence used without the child's knowledge but to the child's benefit.

Case Study 4.2

Coady reports the following research (Hoagwood et al., 1996):

> Four year olds were videotaped playing individually with a research assistant posing as a baby-sitter. A week later half the children met individually with a research assistant posing as a police officer who suggested to them that the baby-sitter the previous week may have done some bad things, and asked for their account of what had happened. Later all the children were questioned by members of the research team. One of the hypotheses in the research as that those who had met with the authority figure would be more likely to say that the baby-sitter had acted badly. (Coady, 2001: 67)

What are your views about this Case Study? Do you think it was ethical? Why? What were the children's rights in this situation?

The rights of research participants

In most educational research, learners' rights are made explicit. Before agreeing to participate, learners should know that they can decide not to participate and that, even if they agree, they can withdraw at any point without detriment to themselves. This can sometimes cause a tension for researchers if the learner does indeed take up the right to withdraw part way through the research and the data collected from that person is then lost to the project. Similarly, there may be tensions, especially when the learners are children or vulnerable adults, if the participant cannot distinguish between the normal practice of giving 'right answers' to teachers' questions and giving their own opinions and thoughts in a research interview (the *Hawthorne effect*). Here the power and status of the researcher must be carefully considered in the planning stage of a research project in order to find ways to minimize this effect. The ethical code under which the research is to be conducted needs to be fully understood by the researcher. In educational research, learners need to be heard and the move towards the use of learners' voices in research has grown in the late twentieth and the twenty-first centuries.

A good example of the pupils' voices being heard is that of Broström and Vilien (1998) who, reporting on their research in Sweden, show how research with children can be ethical by reducing the power of the researcher and valuing the role of the child as 'reflective subject' rather than 'passive object [of research]', by sharing data with them for their comments and even conducting interviews in the child's preferred place 'at the top of a hill' rather than in the head's office.

Planning and executing ethical research

How, then, should educational researchers go about ethically planning and progressing their research?

The first step is to approach the gatekeepers of the education setting in which it is hoped that the research will be set. This is not only courtesy but an ethical matter. Usually researchers write letters and/or information sheets explaining their request in detail with respect to the aims and conduct of the proposed investigation. In cases where access to children and/or vulnerable adults is requested, the informed consent of parents or guardians should also be sought, unless the head or centre manager will act *in loco parentis* (a legal term meaning 'in the place of the parent'). However, it is also important that, even if their parents or guardians give informed consent for children to participate, these prospective participants are asked for their *assent* in a manner appropriate to them, for example, the language used in the request to them.

Throughout the research process, ethical choices will need to be made, such as:

- Have the presumptions and assumptions of the researcher been made explicit?
- Is the sample appropriate?
- Is the research question/hypothesis worthwhile?
- How will the participants and setting be kept confidential and anonymous?
- What type of data collection methods is best suited? (Are interview/questionnaire questions biased or leading?)
- What type of data analysis will be employed? (Will the researcher look for surprises and avoid only looking for what is expected?)
- How will findings be verified/validated? (Will they be trustworthy? Will the participants be involved in the verification?)
- How will the research be reported? (In full or in an edited/way? For what audience?)
- How will the data be kept secure and destroyed once the project is over?

Conclusion

Today, ethical debates involve issues in every aspect of life. The cultural 'clash' between the West and East, technological advances in genetics, medical science, communication and surveillance, destruction of natural habitats and global warming, the rights of individual versus rights of the group, movement by immigrants and refugees, are some of the many contemporary issues that have become the ethical 'zeitgeist'.

It is extremely important, then, that educators clearly adhere to ethical codes of conduct and research processes throughout their work with learners, be they children or adults, in whatever context they interact.

Summary

- ethics is a branch of philosophy
- writers have considered ethical and moral values since the time of Ancient Greece
- modern ethical codes have developed since the atrocities of the Third Reich
- researchers need to be careful throughout their research from planning to reporting to ensure that they follow a good ethical code of practice

- research participants should be party to the ethical considerations of the research in which they are invited to participate – both adults and children

References

Altrichter, H (1993) 'The concept of quality in action research: giving practitioners a voice in educational research', in Schratz, M (1993) (ed.) *Qualitative Voices in Educational Research*. London: Falmer Press

Brostrom, S and Vilien, K (1998) 'Early childhood education research in Denmark', in David, T (1998) (ed.) *Researching Early Childhood Education: European Perspectives*. London: Paul Chapman Publishing

Coady, M M (2001) 'Ethics in early childhood research', in MacNaughton, G, Rolfe, S A and Siraj-Blatchford (eds), *Doing Early Childhood Research*. Buckingham: Open University Press

Cunningham, H (2006) *The Invention of Childhood*. London: BBC

DfES (2003) 'Every Child Matters'

DOH (1991) 'Local Research Ethics Committees'

Hill, M and Tisdall, K (1997) *Children & Society*. Essex: Pearson Education Ltd

HMSO (1989) The Children Act 1989

HMSO (1999) 'Protection of Children Act'

Hoagwood, K, Jensen, P S and Fisher, C B (1996) (eds). *Ethical Issues in Mental Heath Research with Children and Adolescents*. NJ: L. Erlbaum (quoted by Coady, M M (2001) 'Ethics in early childhood research in Mac Naughton', in MacNaughton, G, Rolfe, S A and Siraj-Blatchford (eds), *Doing Early Childhood Research International Perspectives on Theory and Practice*. Buckingham: Open University Press)

Peters, R S (1966) *Ethics and Education*. London: George Allen & Unwin

Schratz, M (1993) (ed.) *Qualitative Voices in Educational Research*. London: Falmer Press

United Nations Convention on the Rights of the Child (UNCRC) (UN 1989)

Wainwright, M (2003) 'Thousands of Pupils in Nationwide Protest', the *Guardian*, 6 March 2003

Further reading

Campbell, A and Groundwater-Smith, S (2007) *An Ethical Approach to Practitioner Research*. London: Routledge

David, T (1998) (ed.) *Researching Early Childhood Education: European Perspectives*. London: Paul Chapman Publishing

Ethics and Education journal published by Routledge, two issues per year also available online

Furrow, D (2006) *Ethics: Key Concepts in Philosophy*. London: Continuum

Grieg, A and Taylor, J (1999) *Doing Research with Children*. London: Sage

MacNaughton, G, Rolfe, S A and Siraj-Blatchford, I (2001) (eds), *Doing Early Childhood Research*. Buckingham: Open University Press

Sevenhuiisen, S (1998) *Citizenship and the Ethics of Care: Feminist Considerations of Justice, Morality and Politics*. London: Routledge

Tansio, T (2002) *Understanding Ethics: An Introduction to Moral Theory*. Edinburgh: Edinburgh University Press

Taylor, M (1998) *Values Education and Values in Education: A Guide to the Issues*. London: Association of Teachers and Lecturers

Although several of these books relate to Early Childhood Education, the principles for ethical research are relevant to research with learners of any age.

Useful websites

www.11million.org.uk/ – This takes you to the home page of 11 MILLION – the Children's Commissioner for England. The website allows you access to their archive, reports, press statements and publications from the UK Children's Commission. The results of consultation with children and young people are placed on this site. There are also links to related sites.

www.bera.ac.uk – British Educational Research Association – contains their ethical code of practice in educational research.

www.bps.org – British Psychological Association; their code of ethical practice is here.

www.brisoc.co.uk – The British Sociological Association: Website contains their ethical code of practice.

www.dcsf.gov.uk – United Kingdom's Department for Children, Schools and Families.

www.globalissues.org – This site covers social, political, economic and environmental issues. There are a number of sections to the website that contain useful information, in particular the 'Human Rights Related Issues'.

www.health.gov.au/nhmrc/ethics – This is an example of ethics from the Australian Health and Medical Research Council.

www.nserc.ca/programs/ethics/english/policy – This website is the Canadian Social Sciences and Humanities Research Council Code of Ethical Conduct for Research Involving Humans.

www.unicef.org – UNICEF is mandated by the United Nations General Assembly to advocate for the protection of children's rights, to help meet their basic needs and to expand their opportunities to reach their full potential. It is guided by the Convention on the Rights of the Child and strives to establish children's rights as enduring ethical principles and international standards of behaviour towards children.

www.tlrp.org.uk – This is the website for the United Kingdom's Teaching and Learning Research Project where teachers involved in the project post their research reports, often these include ethical considerations.

www.savethechildren.org.uk – This is the home page of the UK branch of the charity 'Save the Children'. This charity campaigns and acts as an advocate for children worldwide. They state a focus on four fundamental rights for children: health, freedom from hunger, education and protection.

www.scre.ac.uk – This is the website of the Scottish Council for Research in Education and is another example of a research council's ethical code of practice for educational researchers.

www.uncrc.org – United Nations Charter for the Rights of Children.

Useful internet search terms

ethics
ethical codes
research ethics

Individual philosopher's definitions of ethics can also be found by searching for them by name.

Sociological Perspectives on Education

5

Jon E C Tan and Colin Harrison

Chapter Outline

A social-educational autobiography

Case Study: Philip

Philip is the youngest child of David and Jennie, his sister Sara being older than him by four years and currently studying at Northern University. Though at University, Sara still lives in the family home, a three-bedroomed terraced house on the Pithead estate (a large, mainly local authority housing estate in Wheeltown). For a time, until Philip was six, they had lived with Jennie's parents in a similar house a couple of streets away from their present home. Philip's father, David, came to the United Kingdom from Hong Kong in the mid-1980s, to start an engineering qualification. He had met Jennie, who was also studying on a Health and Social Care course at the same technical college. Sara was a welcome but unexpected arrival and so in 1987 David had cut short his intentions of continuing on to an engineering degree, to take up employment with a local engineering company. Shortly after Philip's twelfth birthday in May 2003, David suffered an industrial injury and since then has been unable to work. Jennie's part-time work as a Care Worker for the local authority and David's disability allowance now provide the main income for the family.

  Philip's secondary school teachers speak of his 'distractions', about his great potential if only he would set-tle and apply himself. In class, he is a bit of the humorist, always ready to make a joke or some observation that raises a smile among his group of friends, but he is sometimes a 'disruptive influence' according to a

⇨

Case Study: Philip—cont'd

number of his school reports. In all honesty (though not known to his teachers), Philip's humour has developed as his way of getting out of 'tricky moments' as he calls them – his reference to his school experiences of bullying, mainly centred on his mixed heritage. Another strategy is not appearing to be 'swotting', at least not in front of his peers. It is a difficult balance to tread what with his family's seemingly constant going on about the importance of getting good grades, getting on. If he had a quid for every time he had heard the words "look at your sister. You'll not get to Uni like Sara, if you carry on like this! Don't know what's happened to you since you went up to the big school." Yes, at primary school, Philip had been praised highly by his class teacher, that is apart from his reluctance to read. It was the sort of books they gave out at school that were the problem. At home he always had more than a couple of books on the go at a time – always about real stuff, not made-up stories. History is still a real passion. So now Philip is 16, waiting for his GCSE results and hoping that they will be better than his mock exams that he failed in spectacular fashion! Even his mates were impressed at how successfully he'd 'bombed out' in Geography.

Viewing the world through a social class lens

Social class: Some difficulties in measurement?

Before studying Philip's autobiography with an analytical focus on social class, it is useful to consider what it is we mean by the term. Social class is a term that conveys a sense of a stratified social organization, one that makes distinctions about society's members based upon a hierarchical model that suggests differences in status. Most commonly and historically, ideas of class have been associated with concepts of economic, occupational status, thus making the connection between that which has a social dimension with the idea that a key indicator of differentiation is economically related. Traditionally then, class has often used occupational information as a means of denoting social class, or socio-economic status. For example, someone with professional, managerial or skilled occupational qualities might be considered to be middle class and those in semi- or unskilled work to be working class. Further iterations of these broad two class groupings have led to the establishment of a number of social classifications based upon occupational data – most commonly being the Registrar General and Hall-Jones scales.

There are, however, significant problems with making connections between a concept of social stratification and a simple occupations-based measure. Where, for instance would someone without a clear occupational location be placed; those people unemployed; those engaged in part-time work or unpaid voluntary work; people with multiple occupations or who change occupations and classifications; those engaged in full-time education; children and young people; the elderly and retired? Once the consideration of the complexity of people's lives in relation to work begins, securely attaching a socio-economic label becomes problematic. Similarly, finding other measures of class has proved equally elusive for social theorists. In the study of compulsory education in the United Kingdom, and elsewhere, it has become common to see a pupils' receipt of free or subsidized school meals (FSM) as a measure of socio-economic class, reinforcing the relationship between 'class', 'wealth' and deprivation. Though there are still significant problems with these measures that involve considerations of FSM and parental occupational details, these are indicators of class that we will carry through this chapter, mainly to provide comparability with studies of class over the years and to enable some reference to governmental statistics.

Considering Philip

Looking at Philip's educational autobiography with reference to social class issues shows that there are a number of indicators within Philip's story to denote a 'working-class' background: Primarily, from Philip's father's occupational details it might be deduced that Philip's background could be broadly considered as working class. There are other factors that also point to such a conclusion that lead to the consideration of economic indicators of the family's income level: David's unemployment; Jennie's part-time semi- or unskilled work; the family's residence in local authority housing. Taken together as indicators of lower socio-economic class (perhaps at most class IIIb, skilled manual, in those scales used most commonly within the United Kingdom), how might this class location impact upon Philip's educational experiences?

As a starting point, government statistics show a significant relationship between a variety of educational 'experiences' and social class. For example, pupils from lower socio-economic backgrounds are more likely to experience lower levels of examination success, achieving fewer grades A–C at GCSE at 16. Looking at Philip's counterparts over the last 35 years or so, it can be seen that pupils from working-class backgrounds – though there have been increases in attainment overall – still find it more difficult than their middle-class peers to secure such grades.

Activity 5.1

What patterns can be identified in the educational attainment of pupils in the United Kingdom at age 16 in relation to socio-economic class?
    Look at the following statistical sources:

    www.statistics.gov.uk
    www.dfes.gov.uk/rgateway

The ways in which social class mediates educational progressions and experiences is not confined to its impact on levels of attainment. Of course levels of attainment are very much an outcome and a close association of social class with other patterns in experiences for children, young people and for that matter adult learners can be seen. In the years of compulsory schooling, for example, pupils from lower socio-economic classes are more likely to truant from school and to experience permanent or temporary exclusions. The inequalities founded on social class lines are similarly stratified when successful entry into further and higher education is considered. The chance of getting in to university, despite government rhetoric about education for all and for life, is still very much weighted in favour of applicants from higher, socio-economic backgrounds – the middle class.

Activity 5.2

With reference to statistical sources for the United Kingdom, is the picture changing?
  Look at the statistical sources again. Consider attainment at 16; also look at the data on social class and entry into Higher Education. Is the relationship any different? Is there a widening or narrowing between lower and higher socio-economic groupings?

If it is a longstanding relationship, then why is it so?

If education is a mechanism for social improvement and change, then why is there the same patterning of experiences in education? A number of authors have put forward theories as to why this may be so. In considering some of them, it is helpful to look at both contemporary and historical texts. Borrowing from what might be broadly considered as a functionalist Marxist perspective, in many factors in the organization of the school system it can be found that disadvantage pupils from working-class backgrounds and that to a great extent the education system operates to replicate the division of labour that is found within later spheres of post-school working life.

Activity 5.3 Longstanding 'structural' Explanations

A number of authors and researchers have attempted to explain the differences in attainment and educational progressions focusing on the school as a middle-class environment that is consequently organized in ways that disadvantage pupils from lower socio-economic origins. Consult the following texts and summarize the main points they make by way of explaining this working-class failure.

Further reading

Ball, S J (1993) 'Education markets, choice and social class: The market as a class strategy in the UK and the USA', *British Journal of Sociology of Education*, Vol. 14(1), 3–19

Bernstein, B (1964) 'Elaborated and restricted codes: Their social origins and some consequences', *American Anthropologist*, New Series, Vol. 66(6), Part 2: The Ethnography of Communication (Dec, 1964), 55–69

Bowles, S and Gintis, H (1976) *Schooling in Capitalist America*. Basic Books: New York

Hargeaves, D H (1967) *Social Relations in a Secondary School*. London: Routledge and Kegan Paul

So it could said that the 'school', or more correctly the education system in the way that it is organized and the ideological messages it communicates 'fail' pupils from working-class backgrounds. Moreover, as attainment at 16 is a significant factor in shaping post-16 destinations (e.g. the continuation and level of educational participation, and difference between 'good careers' and 'dead-end', low-paid work) then such 'failure' casts long shadows over later life-chances. Is it simply then the case that the different patternings of educational progressions can be wholly explained in structural, economic terms and do individuals themselves play any part? What about agency – the active, decision-making individual? Does Philip have any role in shaping his future?

Cultural clashes, meaning and agency

The question of agency and culture were specifically in the forefront of Paul Willis' mind when he set out in the late 1970s to examine the process by which working-class boys made that transition from school to work. In particular, Willis (1977) provides us with an interesting alternative explanation of why and how certain social groupings of young people enter into a particular strata of the labour market, and thus how labour differentiation occurs. Willis, and later Phil Brown (1987), give us a sense that young people's own decision-making is actively involved in this process, in the formation of what Brown calls their 'frames of reference'. For those from working-class backgrounds, what is significant is their perception of the school environment as having little meaning to their future lives. It indeed presents a largely middle-class set of values of deferred reward and meritocratic progression that does not tally with their experiences nor those learned from their families and older social relations. Writers such as Willis provide us with a rich ethnography that suggests that differences in culture and the values contained therein contribute to young people effectively choosing to 'fail' middle-class schooling and what it represents for them.

Activity 5.4 'Failing Yourself?' Paul Willis and Cultural Explanations of Social Class Differences

Willis's argument is that working-class children reject schooling and the values it represents because it has little relevance to their futures. Look at Willis (1977) and Banks et al. (1992) studies. Are there ways in which a subcultural explanation such as Willis's can be a helpful tour in understanding of educational progressions in the changed economic landscape of 1990–2000s?

Social class and Philip reconsidered

In her paper 'Finding or losing yourself', Diane Reay (2001) provides us with a valuable revisiting of the issues of working-class experiences of and relations to education. Class relationships, according to Reay's analysis, are as much a part of understanding educational progressions as they were for Willis (1977). Interestingly, against the backdrop of socio-political constructs of 'failure' and of policy interventions, Reay (2001) demonstrates how notions of 'failure' of being 'a nothing' and being 'found out' within education (2001: 39–41) are internalized by young working-class girls. In this sense, how does education impact upon identities and self-concepts. We will talk about gender later on, but for now let us consider another social factor that carries with it connotations of 'identity' – that of 'race' and ethnicity.

Viewing the world through a race/ethnicity lens

In the above considerations of social class and its impact of educational experiences some difficulties in the conceptualization of 'class' were highlighted and complicit in this, problems in finding robust indicators and ascribing labels. Social class shares such definitional challenges with other social identities such as race and ethnicity. Interesting is it not that two terms have been used here? Broadly speaking, distinctions are made between these terms, the former referring to physical attributes, the latter making reference to cultural factors that people share including, for instance, religious beliefs and customs. These terms are often further confused with that of nationality – legally speaking being a recognized citizen of a nation state. While these distinctions are offered in quite simple terms, hunting out definitions can lead to significant confusion – dictionary definitions for instance tend to define each term by using some of the others, for example:

> A group of people of common ancestry, distinguished from others by hair type, colour of skin, stature, etc. (Collins Concise Dictionary, 1990)

> 1: A human group having racial, religious, linguistic, and other traits in common. 2: Relating to the classification of mankind into groups esp. on the basis of racial characteristics. 3: Denoting or deriving from the cultural traditions of a group of people. (Collins Concise Dictionary, 1990)

Writers such as Balibar and Wallerstein (1991) argue that these terms are used interchangeably because to a great extent they are conceptually interrelated. They are all expressions of 'peoplehood'. Looking at Philip and his family, how such groupings potentially impact upon Philip's educational progressions can be questioned.

Disaggregating educational progressions by race and ethnicity

Issues of race and ethnicity mediate educational progressions in varying ways. From the incidence of truancy and exclusions from school to achievement at 16, when these lenses are used to interrogate educational experiences significant patterns can be identified. For Philip, there is clearly a great emphasis placed upon the importance of education by his family and its value as a means of 'getting on'. At the same time there are messages within Philip's experiences that point to racial bullying as a constant concern for him – to the extent that he has developed quite well-considered strategies in coping. While his major frame of reference outside of school – his family – thus give strong indications of the importance of engaging with education, those within school present difficulties. When considering educational progressions, patterns of achievement can be seen across different social groupings according to race and ethnicity. Consulting national social statistics shows the need to look at different racial and ethnic groupings, rather than treating these as homogeneous categories and experiences. Their experiences of education in terms of achievement are in certain instances quite different.

Activity 5.5

What patterns can be identified in the educational attainment of pupils in the United Kingdom aged 16 in relation to race and ethnicity? How does Philip fare in relation to his peers of different backgrounds?

Look at the following statistics: www.statistics.gov.uk/cci/nugget.asp?id=461

Consultation of the National Statistics for United Kingdom make the following summary with regard to GCSE attainment:

> In 2002 Chinese pupils were the most likely to achieve five or more GCSE grades A*–C in England, with 77 per cent of Chinese girls and 71 per cent of Chinese boys respectively. Indian pupils had the next highest achievement levels: 70 per cent of Indian girls and 58 per cent of Indian boys achieved these levels. The lowest levels of GCSE attainment were among Black Caribbean pupils. Only 23 per cent of Black Caribbean boys and 38 per cent of Black Caribbean girls achieved five or more A*–C grade GCSEs. Pupils from the Other Black, Black African and Pakistani groups had the next lowest levels of attainment. Within each ethnic group a higher proportion of girls than boys achieved five or more GCSE grades A*–C (or equivalent). (National Statistics Online, 2008)

Looking at Philip's experiences in this context is complex. His parents' background gives him an interesting footprint in the world, being of mixed heritage. Certainly when the statistics are interrogated in achievement terms, Philip's Chinese origins may indicate that he is more likely than many minority ethnic groups in the United Kingdom to experience some of the highest levels of attainment at 16. Along with children and young people from India, those of Chinese origins exhibit the highest attainment in the United Kingdom. At the same time it is important to be cognizant of the effects of gender here, and also of his personal experiences of racial bullying. Both these factors can be seen to combine to influence his engagement in education in a number of ways, and his biography mentions his reluctance to draw attention to himself academically among his peers.

Looking at Research: Multiple Factors at Work

Factors such as gender, social class and race/ethnicity may be considered separately as a conceptual starting point. In reality, these influences on educational progressions operate in combination. Afshar and Maynard (1994) and Walker and Barton (1983) considered ways in which gender and race, and indeed social class may be considered as multiple sites of difference.

Hammersley and Woods (1993) also provide a selection of ethnographic accounts that serve as useful examples of how ethnicity and gender are lived out as educational experiences. Also look at:

Ashfar, H and Maynard, M (1994) *The Dynamics of 'Race' and Gender: Some Feminist Interventions.* London: Taylor Francis

Hammersley, M and Woods, P (1993) *Gender and Ethnicity in Schools: Ethnographic Accounts.* London: Routledge

Walker, S and Barton, L (1983) *Gender, Class and Education.* London: Routledge

---

Turning from Philip for a moment, consider some of his peer group: as National Statistics highlight, those young people from Pakistani, Bangladeshi and African Caribbean origins experience less fortunate educational progressions. Such experiences exist at a number of levels, not just being apparent in terms of educational attainment at 16. As the National Statistics information summarizes:

> In 2001/02 Black pupils were more likely to be permanently excluded from schools in England than children from other ethnic groups. The highest permanent exclusion rate was among Black Caribbean pupils, at 42 per 10,000. This was three times the rate for White pupils. Chinese and Indian pupils had the lowest exclusion rates, at 2 per 10,000 and 3 per 10,000 respectively. For all ethnic groups, the rate of permanent exclusions was higher for boys than girls. (National Statistics Online, 2008)

How might differences be accounted for?

Clearly then, viewing educational experiences with a 'race' and ethnicity lens provide further insight into there being patterns of inequalities in the ways in which different social groupings progress through education. As in the considerations above of socio-economic and gender factors, a range of explanations can be offered at different levels of analysis. In accounting for such differences, again the consideration of how those factors at the level of classroom interaction may involve complex processes of labelling about 'ability' and 'intelligence' (Hernstein and Murray, 1994), about notions of challenging and disruptive behaviour and relationships with authority, and about cultures of resistance (Mac an Ghaill, 1988;

Sewell, 1997). At the same time, care must be taken not to lose sight of these inequalities as being patterns of association, replicated time and again, rather than individual occurrences. At the level of the school, the institution and more widely embedded within policy, the differing educational progressions that can be seen through the race/ethnicity lens could be considered as a construct of institutional racism that is bound up in the politics of education, of curriculum, performativity and community. Here the work of Gillborn and Mirza (2000) and Michael Apple (2000) raise interesting questions about how such inequalities can be understood as being institutionalized.

In some of the preceding discussions references to gender have been made as another aspect of social analysis that can be brought to bear on educational progressions has been considered. Similarly, much of the research literature makes clear how issues of social class, race, ethnicity and gender are inextricable entwined.

Viewing the world through a gender lens

Having considered a number of issues which may impact on the performance of Philip, how important is it that he is male? Statistically, Philip is likely to perform less well academically than a girl from a similar family background and set of educational experiences (DfES, 2007; Gillborn and Mirza, 2000).

Since the early 1990s the problem of under-achieving boys has rarely been out of educational debate, yet only 20 years earlier the same debate was taking place about girls' underachievement. Graham Paton, in an article in the *Telegraph* (2007) suggests that even in primary education there is an 'anti-education culture among boys' and that 'the gender gap widens throughout their education'. While the performance gap attributed to gender may not be as significant as that attributed to other social aspects, it continues to increase and it is important to try to identify the causes and possible solutions.

The underachievement of boys is only a relatively recent phenomenon, particularly at secondary level. In the 1970s teachers were still considering how to improve the performance of girls who, at that time, tended to underachieve when compared to boys from similar backgrounds. In 1997, Ted Wragg, writing in the *Times Educational Supplement* noted: 'it is the underachievement of boys that has become one of the biggest challenges facing society today'. (Wragg, 1997). This is a difficult phenomenon to explain. Are there essential biological differences that effect performance? Has the nature of the education and assessment system begun to favour girls? Or is the difference related to changing social conditions?

Consider the biological issues, do they affect the way in which people behave and learn? Just because the woman is the child bearer does this mean that she is the best person to raise the child? Is it implicit in the female make-up that they are better suited for domestic chores and managing a home rather than becoming leaders in professional careers? The potential impact of biological differences has long been a debate; students need to consider whether the culture determines the outcome rather than biological factors. There is a lot of research in this area and while it might not change the impact on educational performance students might consider researching this complex issue in more detail. The web holds many potential sources and the work of Deborah Blum – Sex on the Brain – considers a range of research evidence in this context.

Are these perceptions of the male/female roles simply a hangover from earlier cultural and social constructions that are still entrenched in our modern conception of social order or do they have more definite biological roots? Evidence suggests that this is still the case, that men are disproportionately represented in top jobs and powerful positions. In primary education, only 16 per cent of teachers are male, yet 34 per cent of Head teachers are male (DfES, 2007). Evidence suggests that there is some change in this position but this does not reflect the change in educational performance. Historically the position of women being subordinate to men was reflected in the education system. Girls were not expected to continue in education beyond elementary education, where a family had to make a choice, a son was invariably the one to continue. The 1944 Education Act may have suggested a change in this view, yet there remained fewer opportunities in the system for girls to receive a grammar school education when compared to boys.

Key education reports in the early 1960s continued to reinforce these stereotypes and perceptions. The Newsom Report (1963) on secondary education suggested:

> We try to educate girls into becoming imitation men and as a result we are wasting and frustrating their qualities of womanhood at a great expense to the community . . . in addition to their needs as individuals our girls should be educated in terms of their main social function – which is to make for themselves, their children and their husbands a secure and suitable home and to be mothers.

The Crowther Report (1959) looking at 15–19 education went further:

> The incentive for girls to equip themselves for marriage and home making is genetic . . . . With less able girls schools can and should make more adjustments to the fact that marriage looms larger and nearer in pupils' eyes than it has ever done before . . . her interest in dress, personal appearance and problems of human relations should be given a central place in her education.

Despite this perception, the 1980s saw a shift in educational performance, following pressure within education to improve the performance of girls. This may have been a result of particular educational drives – Girls into Science and Technology (GIST) and Women in Science and Engineering (WISE) – which were designed to change girls' perceptions of what were traditionally male-dominated areas of education and employment. It may also reflect the development of equal opportunities legislation and later the National Curriculum, the former strengthening the rights of girls to choose a wider range of subjects and the latter which prevented girls from opting out of certain subjects' areas. A further issue may be that of the changing social trends for delayed marriage, the need for two wage earners in a family and better childcare provision increasing the potential for girls to have meaningful career aspirations.

Despite these changes and the increasing gap in the educational performance of girls and boys, the stereotype remains firmly entrenched. Natasha Walter reviewing a BBC programme – *The Tattle of the Sexes* – in the *Guardian* (2005) comments:

> People are naturally drawn to those findings that bolster the stereotypes they already hold – and when it comes to sex differences these stereotypes are held with immense tenacity. There have been many changes in the way that men and women behave in family and working life over the last few generations. But obviously a bedrock of inequality remains. Men continue to take more powerful roles in society and women continue to do the bulk of unpaid domestic work and childcare.

It would seem that the stereotype goes against the trend for girls increasingly out performing boys in most areas of education. Research carried out by the University of Edinburgh with 14–16-year-old pupils seemed to suggest that the stereotypes were still present when considering practical situations yet not accepted philosophically. The ideas are summarized as follows:

> In general the young people believed that it was equally important for males and females to get good qualifications at school, to have worthwhile careers and that child care should be a joint responsibility [yet] the views were tempered, however, by the inequalities that they saw around them in the workplace and in their own families. While young people's attitudes may have changed, they are still choosing fairly gender typical subjects at school and aspiring to different types of occupation. Tinklin et al. (2005)

Returning to the underlying biological differences

How can men and women be described? Women are often regarded as passive and not aggressive; care for others; domestic and dependant; easily upset and emotional; dominated by men! Men are active and aggressive; can cope with the world; are logical and unemotional; ought to be able to dominate women! Are these myths, or do they reflect perceptions of men and women in society? What about language, which gender is associate with 'hard', 'gentle', 'affectionate', 'brave'; consider different sayings 'be a man'; 'boys will be boys'; 'as pretty as a picture'; 'as good as gold' – are these descriptions social myths and misunderstanding or a true reflection of roles in society? Pick up an Argos catalogue or visit 'Toys r us' and a delineation between toys for girls and boys is obvious. Is there an innate desire to perpetuate these respective roles or are they really rooted in biological differences? The answer is uncertain but it is important to consider how this impacts on educational performance.

Equal Opportunities Commission (2007) indicates a number of gender differences which are difficult to explain unless biological impacts are accepted.

There is evidence to suggest differences even at pre-school stage, data from the Millennium Cohort Study report (2003) suggests how that 'at the pre school stage, girls have better social and cognitive skills' although this may be explained by evidence that suggests 'Parents are more likely to read and teach songs and nursery rhymes with daughters than sons.'

The report also notes that gender is 'a better predictor than social class and ethnicity of (a child) being classified as having Behavioural, Emotional and Social Difficulty'. The report indicates that 70 per cent of children with Special Educational Needs (SEN) are boys; boys are nine times more likely to be identified as being on the autistic spectrum and four times more likely to suffer from behavioural, emotional and social difficulties (BESD); boys account for 80 per cent of permanent exclusions and 75 per cent of fixed term exclusions. Perhaps this suggests key gender differences which could account for some of the gap in performance.

Within a multicultural society it is also important to recognize groups where the male continues to be regarded as dominant and the women subservient still exist and this can have an increased effect of boys' performance in schools, particularly where the majority of teachers are female. Evidence in 2007 suggests that 84 per cent of teachers in primary schools and 56 per cent of teachers in secondary schools are female (an increasing position) which is often cited as a reason for the underperformance of boys.

While there are clearly issues surrounding the gender differences in performance, the reasons are much more difficult to identify, there are a range of suggestions, but few clear answers. Could it be:

- The 'lad' culture?
- The nature of examinations and particularly coursework?
- The lack of male role models in education?
- The impact of parental attitudes to boys and their place in the family?
- The impact of learning and teaching styles, including teaching materials and books?
- Or, is it still about social condition and perspectives?

Gillborn and Mirza recognize and demonstrate the gender gap as an issue for performance but suggest that 'The gender gap is considerably smaller than the inequalities of attainment associated with ethnic origin and social class background.' (Gillborn and Mirza, 2000: 23). There are clear issues surrounding the difference in performance between boys and girls but does it warrant the high profile it has in discussions on school improvement programmes? The government has recently published the Gender Equality Duty (2007) which seeks to ensure gender equality in all aspects of life; schools are no exception and are expected to 'prepare a scheme identifying gender equality objectives, and setting out the actions it intends to carry out to achieve them'. (Gender Equality Duty, 2007: 21), perhaps this a way forward to achieve gender equality in performance!

Finally, what should the school's role be in this context? Should schools be concerned about perpetuating gender differences or should schools be actively seeking ways to breakdown gender perceptions?

Conclusion

So where does that leave Philip, his family and students of education? In this chapter three of the major social factors that impact upon the educational progressions of children and young people have been considered. While the chapter has focused different analytical lenses on compulsory schooling, that does not imply that it is only in this sphere of education that such social relations and patterns of inequality are played out. Experiences of compulsory education cast long shadows and even a cursory glance at the evidence which brings back into sharp focus the ways in which gender, social class and race and ethnicity affect later progressions of post-16 and beyond. How these pathways extend post-16 have been implied in some of biographical narratives for Philip's family. How have these social factors impacted upon their lives? Can you see patterns in your own?

Summary

In this chapter we have looked at:

- the impact of social perspectives on education.
- views of social class and their impacts on education and development.
- the impact of social issues through the lens of a personal autobiography.
- cultural clashes, meaning and agency, explanations of social class difference.
- viewing the world through a race/ethnicity lens.
- research – multiple factors at work.
- how might we account for differences in educational performance.
- viewing the world through a gender lens.

References

Afshar, H and Maynard, M (1994) *The Dynamics of 'Race' and Gender: Some Feminist Interventions.* London: Taylor & Francis

Apple, M (2000) *Official Knowledge* (2nd edn). London: Routledge

Balibar, E and Wallerstein, I (1991) *Race, Nation, Class: Ambiguous Identities.* London: Verso

Ball, Stephen, J (1993) 'Education markets, choice and social class: the market as a class strategy in the UK and the USA', *British Journal of Sociology of Education*, 14(1), 3–19

Banks, M, Bates, I, Breakwell, G, Bynner, J, Emler, N, Jamieson, L and Roberts, K (1992) *Careers and Identities.* Milton Keynes, Open University Press

Bernstein, B (1964) 'Elaborated and restricted codes: their social origins and some consequences', *American Anthropologist*, New Series, 66(6), Part 2: The Ethnography of Communication. 55–69

Blum D (1997) *Sex on the Brain – The Biological Differences between Men and Women.* New York: Penguin

Bowles, S and Gintis, H (1976) *Schooling in Capitalist America.* New York: Basic Books

Brown, P (1987) *Schooling Ordinary Kids: Inequality, Unemployment and the New Vocationalism.* London: Tavistock

Collins Concise Dictionary of the English Language (2nd edn) (1990) Glasgow, Collins

Crowther Report (1959) *Fifteen to Eighteen*. Department of Education and Science, London: HMSO

DfES (2007) Gender and Education – The Evidence on Pupils in England: Research Paper RTP01–07. Department for Education and Skills

Equal Opportunities Commission (2007) The Gender Equality Duty: Code of Practice, England and Wales. London: HMSO

Garrod, J (2004) 'The education gender gap', *Sociology Review*, 13; pt 4, 26–8

Gillborn, D and Mirza, H S (2000) *Educational Inequality: Mapping Race, Class and Gender*. London: OfSTED

Hammersley, M and Woods, P (1993) *Gender and Ethnicity in Schools: Ethnographic Accounts*. London: Routledge

Hargreaves, D H (1967) *Social Relations in a Secondary School*. London: Routledge and Kegan Paul

Hernstein, R and Murray, C (1994) *The Bell Curve: Intelligence and Class Structure in American Life*. New York: Free Press

Mac an Ghaill, M (1988) *Young, Gifted and Black: Student–Teacher Relations in the Schooling of Black Youth*. Buckingham: Open University Press

Millennium Cohort Study Report (2003) *Millennium Cohort Study – First Sweep 2001–2003*. Centre for Longitudinal Studies

National Statistics Online (2008) http://www.statistics.gov.uk/cci/nugget.asp?id=1388&Pos=6&ColRank=2&Rank=208 (accessed 21 October 2008)

Newsom Report on Secondary Education (1963) *Half our Future*. Department of Education and Science, London: HMSO

Paton, G (2007) 'Boys underachieving at every educational level', *Daily Telegraph*, 11 August 2007

Reay, D (2001) 'Finding or losing yourself? Working-class relationships to education', *Journal of Education Policy*, 16(4), 333–46

Sewell, T (1997) *Black Masculinities and Schooling: How Black Boys Survive Modern Schooling*. Stoke: Trentham Books

Tinklin, T, Croxford, L, Ducklin, A and Frame, B (2005) 'Gender and attitudes to work and family roles: the views of young people at the millennium', *Gender and Education*, 17(2), 129–42

Walker, S and Barton, L (ed.) (1983) *Gender, Class and Education*. London: Routledge

Walter, N (2005) 'The tattle of the sexes', *Guardian*, 16 July 2007

Willis, P (1977) *Learning to Labour: How Working Class Kids Get Working Class Jobs*. Farnborough: Saxon House

Wragg, T (1997) 'Oh boy!', *The Times Educational Supplement*, 16 May 2007

Further reading

Afshar, H and Maynard, M (1994) *The Dynamics of 'Race' and Gender: Some Feminist Interventions*. London: Taylor & Francis

Ball, Stephen, J (1993) 'Education markets, choice and social class: the market as a class strategy in the UK and the USA', *British Journal of Sociology of Education*, 14(1), 3–19

Brown, P (1987) *Schooling Ordinary Kids: Inequality, Unemployment and the New Vocationalism*. London: Tavistock

Gillborn, D and Mirza, H S (2000) *Educational Inequality: Mapping Race, Class and Gender*. London: OfSTED

Mac an Ghaill, M (1988) *Young, Gifted and Black: Student–Teacher Relations in the Schooling of Black Youth*. Buckingham: Open University Press

Reay, D (2001) 'Finding or losing yourself? Working-class relationships to education', *Journal of Education Policy*, 16(4), 333–46

Useful websites

www.dcsf.go.uk/ – Department for Children, Schools and Families: leading work across government in England to improve outcomes for children, including work on children's health and child poverty.

www.esrc.ac.uk/ – Economic and Social Research Council (ESRC): contains useful overviews and research briefings on issues related to education and social research.

www.equalityhumanrights.com/pages/eocdrccre.aspx – Equality and Human Rights Commission: a non-departmental public body (NDPB) established under the Equality Act 2006: contains briefings, statistics and research materials relating to equality and human rights issues, including those concerning education.

www.jrct.org.uk/ – Joseph Rowntree Charitable Trust: A progressive charity organization and funder of social research, including issues concerning power and social justice.

www.jrf.org.uk/ – Joseph Rowntree Foundation: A major Charity funder of social research, with links to past and current research projects, particularly focusing on children and young people.

www.statistics.gov.uk – National Statistics Online: The UK government's official statistics service – contains statistical analysis of social and educational trends.

www.ofsted.gov.uk – Office for Standards in Education (OfSTED): The government's office for inspections and standards in education.

www.ssrc.org – Social Science Research Council (SSRC): A major funder and publisher of research in the field of social science.

www.tda.gov.uk – The Training and Development Agency for Schools (TDA) is the national agency and recognized sector body responsible for the training and development of the school workforce.

Useful internet search terms

social class
social disadvantage
language and social class
culture
cultural capital
gender
race
ethnicity
power and agency

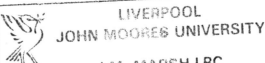

6 Affective Issues in Education

Bridget Cooper

Chapter Outline

Rob and Dad

The significance of emotion in human learning and development

Our lives are a constant process of learning and development – from the first tentative grasps and coos of a baby, to the mastering of the internet by an octogenarian. However, we do not learn in isolation. We are surrounded by other people and inhabit different environments full of natural and man-made phenomena. The learning process involves interacting with all of these, but in particular, with the human beings around us, who form an essential part of the contexts in which we learn. For each new born child there is a whole world to gradually understand. They have to become familiar with their own developing selves and their relationship to the changing world around them. The human species is highly complex and though research informs us about how we develop both as individual organisms and in tandem with others, this learning continues apace.

One powerful aspect of humanity is our affective or emotional nature. We both weep and celebrate when babies are born and when people commit to marriage. We cry when people die but we celebrate and take pleasure in their past lives. We laugh together, sing together, dance together, gasp in awe together, cheer together when goals are scored or victories won and in conflict we get angry and violent with each other. This emotion is both physical and mental in nature. It can be real or imagined and even the imaginary can recreate real feelings. We know that characters in film, television, novels or the theatre are not real, yet we live through their anxieties and excitements as if they really exist. Our pulses race as the tension mounts and we cry or cheer with relief as the drama is resolved.

People have always known the power of emotion in human existence and educators naturally enthuse to share their love of a subject or a skill, to communicate that love with others and imbue them with similar excitement. Research into teacher education and communication stresses the importance of enthusiasm and excitement. We see this daily in the melodramatic nature of most media presenters, who enthuse avidly about their obsessions, whether football, gardening, wild life or cookery, history, music or art. Enthusiasm is infectious.

Further Reading

Damasio, A (1999) *The Feeling of What Happens: Body, Emotion and the Making of Consciousness*. London: Vintage

Damasio, A (2003) *Looking for Spinoza: Joy Sorrow and the Feeling Brain*. London: Heinemann

Goleman, D (1995) *Emotional Intelligence*. London: Bloomsbury

Kyriacou, C (1986) *Effective Teaching in Schools*. Hemel Hempstead: Simon and Schuster

Strangely, the affective or emotional aspects of learning have often been neglected by academics in favour of the process of thinking or cognition. Yet in some contexts we use the concepts of thinking and feeling interchangeably, for example, *I feel/think this is important.* We naturally speak of our instincts and our intuitions, our loves and hates, being turned on and off by different people or subjects, yet it is surprising that not more research has been done into the emotional aspects of learning. However, the intangible nature of emotion makes it difficult to research and its association with feminist thinking has rendered it less popular in the male-dominated academic world than perhaps it should be. However, in recent years, the significance of emotion has been officially recognized in schools through the Excellence and Enjoyment agenda (DfES, 2003) and in the learning of teachers (Hoban, 2002). The significance of emotion to learning is a vital reason to investigate it and understand it deeply. The following section explains what research reveals about our current understanding.

Activity 6.1

Consider your own learning, both formal and informal. Identify any aspects which you really enjoyed or really disliked.

Can you identify the factors which produced that positive or negative reaction in you?

What was it about these particular learning episodes which turned you on or off?

Were the effects of these episodes long lasting or short term in terms of your learning and development? Do you still like or dislike certain subjects or activities as a result?

What part did human relationships play in your learning?

Theory of education – the role of affect

The whole area of the emotions has been avoided and according to some even scorned by many academics (Damasio, 1999; McCarthy, 2000). However, exciting technological developments in neuroscience and increased understanding of the workings of the brain have changed this. This research (Damasio, 1999; Goleman, 1995; Maclean Hospital, 2001; Narvaez, 2007; Watt, 2000) reconfirms the significance of the emotional in personal and academic development, recognized in the psychological literature of the 1960s and 1070s (Aspy, 1972; Rogers, 1975), but which lost favour in the more mechanistic approaches to teaching in the late 1980s and 1990s.

Since human relationships are intrinsic to educational processes and are emotional in nature, we need to understand more about how humans share and communicate their thoughts and feelings. In particular the concept of 'empathy' appears to be central to the understanding of affect in education since it enables human beings to share understanding. The New Oxford Shorter English Dictionary (1993 edition) suggests that empathy comes from the German word *Einfühlung* describing it as, *the power of mentally identifying oneself with (and so fully comprehending) a person or object of contemplation* (1993: 808).

Philosophers and educationalists have recognized the role of emotion in human relationships from Aristotle onwards. In the eighteenth century Hume used the word 'sympathy' in a similar sense to the current definition of empathy and stated that we have a natural propensity 'to sympathize with others and to receive by communication their inclinations and sentiments' (Hume, 1739: 316). For Marks and Engels (1888) over a century later, man could only reach his human potential, not as an individual but as a social being, in his relations with his fellow men and women. The denunciation of individualism, and *naked self-interest*, is at the heart of his critique of capitalism. Human relationships are not just rational or functional but sensual and personal and make us complete. He talks of man acquiring the world through his senses and his relationships with others making him whole (Fischer, 1973).

In the twentieth century, Macmurray (1935: 43) talks of the importance of emotions and sensitive awareness, of employing the senses for the sheer joy they give us, rather than utilizing them for narrower intellectual purposes. He sees the intellect as being subordinate to the emotions and self-centred rather than other-centred. He believed that sensual sensitivity brings human beings together, as the root of human communion and religion, whereas Marks and Engels (1988) believed the supreme form of human integration and interaction was communism. Both saw human relationships and interaction as the pinnacle of humanity. Hay (1997) links Marx's concept of the 'species-being' to the idea of spiritual awareness to heightened sensitivity and suggests that this awareness, which Noddings (1986) calls *receptivity* and Watson and Ashton (1995) call *openness*, is actually a physical state. These descriptions define empathy as a neurobiological state or process, where mind and body function in tandem, opening up to process incoming information from outside the self.

The significance of empathy

Empathy was avidly researched in the 1960s and early 1970s. The influence of Rogers on the role of empathy in counselling and education was significant. Rogers defined empathy in this way: 'it means to sense the hurt or pleasure of another as he senses it and to perceive the causes thereof as he perceives them' (1975: 3). He also argues, 'that empathy dissolves "alienation" and "values the other person and their world, accepts the person as he is" with the consequence that they value themselves and are able to open up to others' (ibid.: 5–6). Later he interchanges the term *empathy* with *sensitive understanding* and explains how this enables even very disturbed individuals to feel valued. Marks and Engels (1888) argued that people become alienated in a capitalist system where financial links replaced human relationships. Market values embedded in education systems seem to limit empathic relationships (Cooper, 2004, 2007).

Empathy creates a mutual bond and is signified by what Noddings (1986) calls '*engross-ment*', being totally concerned for the well-being of another. For both Rogers and Aspy, empathy was a common human quality, which could be developed and improved by train-ing. Aspy developed training in empathy for student teachers (Rogers, 1975). Hargreaves (1972) called for empathy training to ensure 'caring' teachers and such training has been conducted more recently, in Italy for example (Francescato, 1998). This of course raises some interesting issues, if empathy actually develops early in human relationships as Goleman (1995), Leal (2002) and Bowlby (1951) suggest, can training really develop empathy?

There is some consensus that empathy is easier in interactions with someone like your-self (Rogers, 1975; Schantz, 1975). Generally (though not exclusively) children find it easier to empathize with other children, boys with other boys and so on. Kozeki and Berghammer (1992) identified different levels of empathy, distinguishing between the empathy shown by a salesman, who aims to understand you to close a sale and the empathy of a leader for example, who has the long-term interests of his team at heart.

The influence of Rogers' work on 'empathy' and its pertinence to teaching, learning and human development, has permeated educational thinking worldwide (Brandes and Ginnis, 1990; Pike and Selby, 1988). It holds particular significance in the area of pastoral educa-tion, special needs and multicultural education, where perhaps a higher degree of empathy is needed, simply because of the diversity of pupils with particular needs, or for pupils from different regions, races, religions and cultures. Cooper (2002) found that high levels of empathy enabled teachers to understand those who were very different from themselves, for instance children with special needs. However some teachers only demonstrated empathy with certain students not with others, revealing the nature of prejudice.

Goleman (1995) suggests that the receptivity needed for empathy is restricted if the per-son is already too emotional. The flooding of the brain with one emotion can upset the ability to tune into others. Damasio (1994) argues that emotions are vital to complex learn-ing and decision-making, therefore an ability to tune into emotions is needed to support learning. Cooper (2002) argues that when teachers' minds are absorbed by schemes of work, targets and content, they are less able to enter the minds of their pupils and address their needs appropriately.

Empathy assumes a whole-person approach to learning but the dominance of a mechanis-tic, curriculum-based approach to education in the 1980s and 1990s has largely ignored this whole-person approach (McCarthy, 2000; Priestley, 2000). Best (2003) argued that affect-ive issues have been largely ignored in the British education system for decades. However, recently affect has been considered more seriously in education via government policies such as Excellence and Enjoyment (DfES, 2003) and Every Child Matters (HMSO, 2003). Emotional intelligence is considered important, even if its development constitutes another addition to the already overburdened curriculum.

These recent changes stem from research in neuroscience, values development and even artificial intelligence, all of which have reaffirmed the significance of the role of emotions in learning and development. Leal (2002) discussed the ability of babies to respond to emotion in others, and Winkley (1996) explained how the neural networks in the brain grow when the baby feels accepted and cared for. The works of Damasio (1994) and Goleman (1995) are typical summaries of research into brain development and link the emotional, the cognitive and physical as never before. They show that 'rational' decisions are inextricably linked to our inner feelings and physical processes.

Damasio (1999) explains the significance of intense interaction and engagement in learning, where the senses are focused on the object or person of interest. He emphasizes the role of the human's own sense of body and self, in relation to the world he perceives. At each interaction a human recreates his image of self (body and brain) in the mind. With each positive interaction, the sense of self is continually reinforced and updated and the person is encouraged to open up more, explore more and learn more. Negative interaction causes the brain and body to retract and protect itself.

With positive multi-sensory interaction, the brain and body absorb information rapidly becoming more engaged, and better able to understand. This absorption applied to people resembles Noddings' engrossment (1986). When one empathizes, one becomes engrossed in other people, absorbing and responding to feedback. Empathy involves learning intensely about others and sharing both their cognitive and emotional responses, creating an internal mental model of them, which relates closely to one's own. This total engrossment is how parents relate to new babies and how people who fall in love relate to each other. Damasio (1999) explains the universality of emotion in human beings, which implies that all people can relate to each other at these deeper levels. Love is at the heart of these ideas but it is a concept that has proved problematic for highly rational academics.

Conversely, particular brains and certain brain damage ensure fewer links between emotional and rational thinking, and can reduce the ability to create an internal representation of the outer world. Such people struggle to perceive the world as others do, changing their ability to understand the effects of their actions on others, resulting in less inhibited and more antisocial behaviour (Damasio, 1994, 1999; Goleman, 1995; Sacks, 1985, 1996). Even verbal aggression can seriously damage the brain and its capacity to learn (Maclean Hospital, 2001).

Empathy in teaching and learning

Given this newer neurological evidence of the significance of affect in learning and development, the question of what empathy looks like in learning situations is crucial. In terms of teacher empathy Kyriacou (1986) speaks of, 'the importance of teachers being able to see the lesson from the pupils' perspective' (p. 113) and explains it is a significant contributory factor in all eight of the teacher characteristics, seen in the effective teacher.

Cooper (2002) investigated in detail the nature of empathy in interactions in learning and found different types, which we will now explore: fundamental, profound, functional and feigned. These were directly affected by the learning contexts and involved both cognitive and affective factors. Empathy involved creating a rich mental model of others, both factual and emotional, with which to interact. This sits comfortably with Vygotsky's emphasis on human relationships in learning (1976) and the inseparability of cognition and affect (1986).

Fundamental empathy

Fundamental empathy was used to initiate or facilitate social relationships, for example the sort of friendly interaction made in passing at the supermarket checkout. Pleasant interaction in the daily course of events makes life run more smoothly. Fundamental empathy was used naturally by teachers to initiate relationships and had two key categories described below.

Initial characteristics

To begin to form relationships empathic teachers adopt a non-judgemental approach. This means being acceptable and open in their beliefs and attitudes, paying close attention to the feelings and thoughts of others, listening carefully, showing signs of interest and engagement in their conversation or actions, being very positive in verbal and non-verbal communication and showing enthusiasm both for the content and process of interactions and the person involved. Teachers associate empathy both with giving attention and being attentive. When attention is focused between pupils and teacher, engagement and communication are maximized. Any distraction or problems, fear or anxiety reduces positive attention. If teachers model empathic behaviour, students emulate it and positive emotion spreads improving the learning ambience.

Means of communication

Clear facial expression and positive interaction are very important. Eye contact leads to rapid and meaningful communication and along with smiles, nods and a forwardly inclined posture, ensures attention and allows greater understanding to be transferred between teacher and pupil. The teacher's face can be used expressively to emphasize both content and feeling during conversation. This encourages sharing of understanding, further interaction and then students emulate this behaviour in their interactions. Close observation of students' non-verbal reactions inform the teacher about their feelings. Teachers are able to switch emotions rapidly. Any negative display to correct behaviour transforms rapidly into positive emotion to maintain a positive climate.

Within this category *gestures and body language* help to clarify and illuminate conversation engaging curiosity. Movement combined with bodily expression or physical rearrangement of the room engages interest and emotion, drawing students into the interaction. *Height and distance* are also significant. Physical distance seems to be symbolic of emotional distance. Though teachers stand up and move away from the class to address the whole group, closeness and equality of status is important for individual communication. Sitting beside students or lowering their body position improves communication, although teachers are aware of some students' negative feelings about close contact. *Language and voice tone* are very important. Teachers use appropriate language for the level of the student, and reflect their student's style of language before developing and extending vocabulary. Varied voice tone adds emotion and drama, bringing interaction and topics to life.

Many teachers are expert communicators and can rapidly generate good relationships. However, these often function on a superficial level, especially when they teach many students infrequently. More detailed knowledge of students is a feature of the deeper level of empathy described below.

Profound empathy

Over time, and with frequency of interaction, fundamental empathy can become profound, signified by deeper levels of understanding and higher quality relationships which involve frequent positive interaction and mutual respect. Profound empathy facilitates excellence in teaching and learning and involves many complex interrelated facets.

Teachers demonstrating profound empathy understand their students as complex individuals functioning within different environments who have complex relationships with other teachers, peers and family. Teachers modelled a very caring, personalized, almost parental approach. This research confirmed and illuminated the powerful effects of profound empathy on self-esteem which in turn supports learning. Empathic teachers are revealed as highly moral individuals who attach themselves mentally and emotionally to their students and generate similar responses in return. Positive personal interaction supports high levels of engagement and in positive relationships teachers assess their students more effectively and make higher demands.

The most positive relationships and learning are seen where teachers work one to one, as with English as an Additional Language and Special Educational Needs support. Here the emotions become increasingly positive, resulting in happiness, fun and humour in interaction. Advice and constructive criticism become much more effective in a generally positive, trusting atmosphere. Empathic teachers give time and sole attention, especially to students who need it more. They understand the necessity of physical contact for many children and they create a relaxed, comfortable and informal context for learning.

Empathic teachers know themselves well, are very human and fallible in the classroom drawing on their own childhood experiences, and sharing aspects of their personal lives with students. Through this they equalize relationships and permit imperfection, while encouraging positive attitudes to life and learning. They seek to understand learners deeply and explain 'why' rather than simply 'what'. They support social and emotional as well as academic development, believing they are all interrelated.

Profoundly empathic teachers treat students as unique individuals, valuing their existing knowledge and development and building on it. They treasure difference rather than normative comparison so that students, whatever their level, are encouraged to develop.

They create resources and environments which make learners feel confident and secure but which interest and challenge them. Their emotional closeness to students leads empathic teachers to care deeply for them, to seek solutions to their needs, to sacrifice themselves for their sake, to protect them and to perceive the whole person more deeply. They see themselves as bridges of understanding between young people, other adults, parents and community and have a holistic view of individuals and their worlds. Students reciprocate their care and enact it with others, creating a more empathic ambience in classrooms. Where teachers have the opportunity to develop profound empathy, behaviour and learning can be transformed. They create an extremely rich mental model of individuals in their minds, which they can relate to closely, both emotionally and cognitively. They draw on all their life experience and the clues emanating from pupils to interpret their feelings and understanding. The following quotations give a flavour of what empathic teachers believe and practice. It begins with knowing students as individuals and by name.

> [I]f you don't know somebody's name how can you ever make a connection to have any understanding of what's behind the physical presence of the person. (Sara)

> [Empathy] is being sensitive towards the needs of the child trying to, trying to treat each one of those as a little human being as opposed to a pupil. So they all have different needs, different attitudes that I've got to be very much aware of. (Anna)

> I mean I do love children when it comes down to it. (Anna)

Giving time was symbolic of care, made students feel valued, created more equal relationships and deeper understanding:

> Well you'd think that the most important thing that you can ever give anybody in life is time – is your time for them. (Claire)

The more relaxed and natural the teacher could be, the more fun they could have. Then lessons and learning were enjoyable. This was especially important for special needs students:

> I take in all sorts of games . . . anything that makes them laugh really. And I really feel I've got to get them totally relaxed and not worried (Anna).

Developing positive emotions sometimes involved initially masking negative emotions since finding affinity with less likeable children was central to empathy.

> It's a bit more forced, the smiling and everything in that situation, because that child isn't automatically making you feel like that. You know that you'll find some point of contact with the child and something the child's interested in and then work from there. (Mary)

Profound empathy incorporates a deep understanding of self and others which appreciates all existing and historical relationships and their impact on learning. It includes the ability to understand a wide range of students and to take responsibility for their needs. Empathic tutors have a richly adaptive and integrated concept of themselves and others. They build a student's self-esteem and self-worth, create emotional links between tutor and student and build trust and security. This emotional closeness enables the tutor to discover hidden factors, which might enhance or inhibit learning both inside and outside school and enable them to be sensitive to and respond to changes in children's lives. The development of trust and security also allowed risk taking in learning: 'If they feel secure with somebody, they're going to have an attempt at a word they can't read or have a go' (Charlotte).

Profound empathy is not a sentimental concern for the other. It involves genuinely taking a real interest, getting to know and understand lots of factors in a person's thinking and feeling. When two people know each other very well, they can be more honest and more supportive. The constructive criticism vital for learning, is more successful in positive relationships, where the person is well known. Sensitive understanding can challenge and change prejudice or inaccurate conceptions.

The teachers aimed to extend the positive climate out into the home wherever possible: 'you instill them (parents) with confidence and importance about their child.' (Claire). Sharing positive visions of their futures with students and their parents could fill them with expectations: 'There's a world out there! Fill them with ideas and fantasies and dreams and hopes and aspirations . . . then they'll be able to [do this] themselves, won't they'. (Claire).

Real depth of attunement and understanding was only seen in one-to-one and small group situations. These teachers understood that sole attention makes children feel valued and important: 'so you've got to give that sole concentration . . . [ ] otherwise she's not worthy'(Claire). One-to-one attention could transform behaviour and support learning:

> I'm building a better relationship with this boy than I ever do in the class cos he won't say anything, but in here, (withdrawal group) where he feels quite happy and relaxed and he's saying a lot more and we're having a giggle together, I feel as if we're getting on, building up a lot better rapport (Anna – reporting a teaching assistant's comments).

A very positive aspect of our human need for empathy is that many children will seek out a trusting empathic relationship. They want and need 'attention'. 'Attention seeking' children are rarely classrooms criminals, they have a developmental need.

Functional empathy

Functional empathy was an adaptation of empathic behaviour for large classes where teachers form a mental model of the group for the purposes of interaction. They attune to the group, their interests, and their attainment level. This enables the teacher to create a rapport and to plan for and support learning. However, this type of empathy is not sufficiently personalized to be really effective for individuals. Many students are not known well enough to make good progress, mainly due to the limited time available for individual interaction. By having this mental model of a group for interaction, teachers model stereotyping and have to manage and control behaviour rather than exemplifying it. For example, they need rules about listening when others are talking, because there are too many students for them all to have a chance to speak.

Many teachers combine functional empathy with a more profound kind whenever an opportunity arises for individual interaction or when relationships recur with students over time. Though this can be effective in primary school, it is harder in secondary school or in higher education because of the limited interaction time any teacher has with any particular student in what is essentially a fragmented curriculum. A-level groups and postgraduate groups, however, usually have better ratios and allow more personal interaction.

Feigned empathy

Feigned empathy was shown when people pretend to be sensitively understanding but in reality think and later behave, quite differently. This is exemplified by the deceit of the con-man who charms you to eventually defraud you, or the frightening mock charm of the child-abuser who grooms a child with false kindness, before violating them. The pretended sensitivity shown initially is a temporary performance, designed ultimately for self-interest. Fraudsters and psychopaths can be frighteningly adept at feigning empathy for their own ends and have usually had such deceit modelled to them.

Constraints on empathy in the educational system

Different learning contexts and factors in the hidden curriculum (the unintentional learning in schools) affect the degree of empathy which can be shown by teachers. Alienation and disaffection presents itself often as a strange feeling of detachment or worthlessness, but it is difficult to identify the cause when it is created by the hidden curriculum. Often it is caused by the absence of good relationships.

In many contexts the frequency of individual interaction remains at a low level. The fragmented, infrequent nature of relationships in some years in secondary schools and some university undergraduate courses, limits the quality of relationships and restricts the opportunity to offer adequate care and support for individual learning. Lack of time for individuals, large classes and an over-filled, fragmented curriculum, fragments and degrades learning relationships. Unempathic managers or policies, a poor working environment and large numbers of needy students reduce the ability of teachers to be empathic. One very needy child can effectively monopolize the teacher's empathy. Many needy children in a class can compound the problem. Empathy requires mental space to accommodate students' perspectives, which is difficult when you are absorbed by many other agendas or are anxious about student behaviour. Creativity, imagination, deep-thinking and reflection require time and space and are closely related to empathy. These facets of learning are more difficult to develop in large classes. Students in large classes are obliged to compete for the one adult resource at the expense of other students; this also reduces their empathy and degrades the classroom climate.

Functional empathy is much more evident in classrooms than profound empathy and is a by-product of working with large groups. The need to manage the group produces an unequal power relationship which eats away at the climate of mutual respect and often replaces positive affect with fear or disdain. Large classes oblige a teacher to become less empathic, to resort to techniques, tricks and rituals rather than communicating openly and in a mutually respectful way with individual pupils.

Teachers' examples of constraints on empathy are shown below. When these factors occur in combination (as they almost always do) they will necessarily mathematically reduce the quality of empathy. A support teacher working one to one with a child for three hours a week is likely to have sixty times more frequency of interaction, than secondary teachers teaching that child in a class three times a week. The magnitude of the problem is embedded in these simple numbers. How often does an individual student get listened to? What time do teachers have to model thoughtful argument by hearing all contributions? Where is the time to develop critical, creative and collaborative thinking? However much teachers value such ideas, they struggle to enact and model them in the time frames and class sizes within which they work.

Class size

The most powerful factor in reducing empathy is class size. More children means more group interaction, thus on a daily basis teachers model stereotyping, potentially a moral and educational disaster. This issue is aggravated in the depersonalized timetables of secondary schools and in anonymous lectures in universities.

> [O]ver-faced with hundreds of faces who all can look the same on the first sort of appearances. It takes a long time to get to know them, so then it's harder to break down those inaccessible groups. (Sara – secondary)

Insufficient time

Teachers linked poor ratio to lack of time and some individuals need more time than others.

> you never have enough . . . you never have enough time . . . time to speak to the kids as much as you want because you have always got everybody to think about I suppose class size comes into it . . . the more children you've got the more you've got to look after. (Margaret – primary)

> You've got a 45-minute lesson, what am I expected to spend on average – two minutes with a kid. They need more than two minutes. (Will – secondary)

Endless tasks beyond the classroom also limit time. There is minimal time to exchange understanding with parents, to mark work in detail, to share understanding with other staff, and with outside agencies. Primary staff develop more detailed knowledge of children through frequency of contact and continuity in smaller environments but secondary school teachers find it difficult even to learn names. Teachers struggle to find individual time although they know its effect on attitudes, behaviour and achievement:

> He's always causing trouble and at times a very nasty child and not one you could immediately put your arms round . . . but saying that there are times if he's on a one-to-one with you and he wants the attention and he loves that attention and he'll talk and he's a different child. (David)

Curricular problems

With the over-filled curriculum, even primary teachers dominate the delivery and struggle to find time for the personal dialogue and interaction associated with empathy: 'it's hard at times to be on an individual level with the children – there's so much to get through in a week'. (Frances – primary)

In secondary schools with large classes and infrequent contact, especially in years seven to nine, relationships are fragmented along with the curriculum and for many students failure in the normative assessment regime is inevitable: 'I think the National Curriculum, although it is good in many ways, is a disaster for the lower kids'. (Will – secondary)

Teacher quality

To cope with the demands of the system teachers have to be highly skilled, resilient and persistent. Some situations are much more difficult and some teachers cope better than others. Degree quality was considered less important than empathy by the head teacher in this study. Talking about a teaching assistant he said, 'she knows what to do and when best to do it . . . she is magical – I've come across people with damm good degrees who can't teach at all'. (Terry)

The make-up of individuals and groups

The nature of individual children and groupings, have an effect on the teacher's ability to show empathy. Some children need more teacher time, leaving less time available for others. Children with little empathy themselves require the most empathy. They find large classes impossible and need one-to-one support. In classes with many needy children, teachers struggle to meet all their needs.

> I've got one year seven class with eight children with IEPs, statements – they're all vying for attention and within the course of a lesson if you are going to deliver the facts, try and assess everybody and then check at the end that it's all gone in, the time for actual individual – [ ] that time is reduced because you're spending time with other stuff. (Fay – secondary)

The physical environment

Teachers needed space, appropriate rooms and appropriate resources and equipment. Large numbers in small classrooms and the accompanying noise levels, meant teachers were sometimes thwarted in their attempts to know children deeply and had to focus on management and more negative interactions.

Unempathic management and inappropriate policies

Some managers, also restricted in their actions by factors above, found no time for knowing or valuing their teachers and pursued unempathic behaviours and policies which frustrated teachers. School or government policies which stress standardized assessment and competition create a competitive atmosphere in which some children feel devalued and some teachers and managers and other children learned to treat less successful children with disdain. This could result in 'institutional empathy removal'. (Sara)

These seem to be some of the most pressing issues which need addressing in education. If empathy is intrinsic to learning and excellent teaching, we all need to argue for the provision of conditions in which it can thrive.

Activity 6.2

Take an opportunity to identify a student who behaves badly in a large classroom or group. Observe them in class and then in a one-to-one support lesson. Write a detailed account of the occasion, what they did and the nature of their attitude, behaviour and interactions. Do you observe any differences between the two sessions?

Activity 6.3

Spend time talking with a child who has problems in school and find out a little about their home life. What do you feel are the connections between the two?

How do we address emotional issues in schools today?

Thankfully in recent years affect in learning is taking a more prominent role. Emotional intelligence has become a favoured topic and a whole range of initiatives have sought to promote this in children. Organizations such as Antidote are working hard to support institutions in the understanding and support of emotional development. Nurture groups have been established in many schools to support the most emotionally needy children. Circle time encourages the expression of individual feeling. However the philosophy behind these initiatives often conflicts with the more rigid target and assessment-driven nature of the main school curriculum. Children with multiple psychological and emotional needs are still some times treated as if their behaviour can be remedied by a simple detention.

Further Reading and Useful Websites

Goleman, D (1995) *Emotional Intelligence.* London: Bloomsbury

Macgilchrist, B, Myers, K and Reed, J (2004) *The Intelligent School,* London: Sage

www.antidote.org.uk/ – **Antidote** works with schools to help shape learning environments where everyone is motivated and able to participate.

www.dfes.gov.uk/behaviourimprovement/nurture/index.cfm – Nurture groups are small groups usually with younger children in schools, where children with emotional needs get extra care and support from teachers who model good relationships and build trust to support the child's emotional, social and intellectual development.

www.jennymosley.demon.co.uk – The Whole School Quality Circle Time Model. Has a commitment to building children's sense of self-worth and helping them to care more about the feelings of those around them.

Nevertheless new courses for middle management and headship in schools do address the literature from neuroscience and concepts of empathy are well-embedded in health and social services, which also have developmental and educational roles. However curriculum and training initiatives will have limited value, if it is the hidden curriculum which teaches children about how they are valued and affects how they feel about learning. Government policies which disregard this may ensure that schools remain emotional deserts for some children.

More time for individuals is needed to develop empathic relationships in schools. Class sizes need to be reduced dramatically and time funded for interaction between parents and teachers in order to create a virtuous circle of positive feeling and shared understanding. Particular resources need to be focused on those with the greatest need and all students could benefit from individual tutoring or mentoring. Understanding and supporting parents and helping them to understand and support their children's learning are a very important to optimizing learning and development. Sure Start provision (2007) is beginning to have an impact on children's learning and we need to build on this. It is the human support which will most effectively improve the affective dimension in schools. The profound empathy needed for excellent teaching requires time and frequency to develop. More needy students need more time because they have often multiple, complex issues to support and resolve. Profound empathy is precisely the quality which enables the current government requirement for personalized learning.

The combination of high-quality human support alongside well-designed technological support can be particularly effective for learning and the more equal relationships facilitated by technology can be more empathic (Cooper and Brna, 2003). The large interactive whiteboards with their multi-sensory appeal can be very engaging and stimulating when used interactively and the pictures, colours, animation, sound and music can vastly increase the quality of non-verbal interaction, which is a key aspect of profound empathy. However if the use of Interactive white boards (IWBs) leads to an overemphasis on whole class teaching and more teacher domination it will still make classroom relationships teacher-centred, rather than pupil-centred. A 'one size fits all' approach runs counter to an empathic approach and uses functional rather than profound empathy in interactions. The arrival of virtual learning environments may help to enhance communication between schools, parents and children but the technology will not replace face-to-face contact which breeds trust, human concern and emotional bonding. (Cooper, 2007)

Teacher education

Student teachers are quite likely to be highly empathic in nature (Cooper, 2002), but the conditions in which they are trained in universities and in which they eventually work, can make it difficult to experience or demonstrate profound empathy. It may be a serious cause of the continued early exodus from the profession. Educational leaders who fail to support empathic staff may also drive them to search out alternative careers.

Ideas for best practice

All contexts are different and strategies need to be adapted to suit the individual participants and the immediate environment. However, in terms of emotional development several behaviours and strategies can be identified to support it.

Regular individual and positive personal interaction

This is the key ingredient in successful affective education and supports mutual respect, care and 'love' of each other. Knowing students very well enables teachers to most effectively meet needs and make them feel confident and valued. It enables teachers to assess them effectively, plan appropriately for their learning in both content and approach, feedback to them most effectively and develop them rapidly. Individuals need to build trust with key people before they can comfortably interact with a range of others. Finding time for personal interaction can be difficult but teachers and schools need to build this in wherever possible, in both informal ways through human conversations, clubs and other activities and through more small group activity where adults work side by side with children but also through regular one-to-one chats to ensure all children get to know and be known by their teacher. Schools have found time for planning and preparation. They now need to find time for people.

One-to-one conversation at an early stage in a relationship leads to greater emotional attunement more rapidly. This enables teachers to learn not to judge the child but find time to understand them. A simple, friendly more understanding conversation can transform a child's behaviour and their personal state from angry and aggressive to happy and cooperative. Conversations about topics beyond school can often help. Finding out the child's interests outside the classroom can be very motivating. If they have negative emotional baggage which they bring to school gained either from past school experiences, or from home life, this needs to be transformed into positive emotions. Talking to them about what they like, what interests and motivates them, changes the teacher's relationship from a negative managerial one into a positive human one. In this sense teachers may have to forget about the curriculum for a while in order to meet the child's specific needs. Creating high-quality relationships with each individual will enable the whole class climate to be more caring, creative and productive.

Avoiding the public comparison of children will ensure that they do not feel inferior and value their particular progress as opposed to their progress in relation to others really helps. Good teachers value each step in a child's progress and these should be valued in public and shared with other staff and parents wherever possible to create a virtuous circle of good feeling. Negative labelling should be avoided at all costs. Praise and positive verbal and non-verbal communication in copious quantities is very effective.

Pair or small group interaction

Small groups are in general more emotionally supportive to work in than large groups. They enable people to open up, to have an opportunity to speak, to have time to listen to each others' perspective and to iron out misunderstandings. Pair work and small group work can be very powerful in this regard. However, the nature of the participants and the culture in the environment can make a difference. Children can be encouraged to listen and to share but some, because of their nature and experience, may find it easier than others. Knowing each individual enables a teacher to make a good selection of partners. Careful observation followed by teacher intervention will ensure appropriate support and progress.

It is important however to recognize that some children simply need very sensitive one-to-one support and have not the self-esteem or social skills to cope with group work and large classroom situations. Teachers need to recognize this and request specialist support at an earliest opportunity while continuing to work hard to build a trusting relationship with the child themselves.

Larger groups

Working with larger groups is less effective but teachers often have no choice. Skilled teachers can manage interaction in larger groups, for example a class of 30, but have minimal time to interact with individuals. Unstable or highly divergent groups can be harder to manage as this means even greater need to know individuals. Whole class interaction will always be inappropriate for some if not many of the children. For example, whole class phonic work around the phoneme 'sc' might be very relevant for five pupils in the class and either too difficult or too easy for all the others, resulting in either loss of self-esteem or boredom. Teachers often remain unaware of how inappropriate some teaching is for particular members of the group since they need to interact individually in order to know this. Disaffected behaviour might indicate a problem but often results in negative interaction directed at the pupil.

Utilizing a wide range of teaching strategies that incorporate creativity, drama, music, art, ICT, practical and physical activity, alongside more traditional tasks will allow every child in a class to shine in some aspect and help build their self-esteem which will impact on other aspects of their learning. Sensitivity to their low esteem in relation to some subjects (maths is a common one) and gentle encouragement with appropriate tasks and scaffolding can change their feelings about themselves in relation to these subjects and really boost self-esteem.

Teacher enthusiasm is key to large class teaching. In order to engage everyone and maintain the cohesion of the class, teachers need to be exciting, dynamic and good-humoured while simultaneously being caring and supportive, they need to be able to be both an upfront performer and a sensitive personal assistant using functional empathy but making opportunities for profound empathy whenever possible.

Having a class very regularly or every day will support better individual relationships than once a week for example, because you will recognize uniqueness and have opportunities for personal as well as group interaction. In secondary schools senior staff need to work on reducing the fragmentation of the curriculum and timetabling the teachers to teach across subjects in blocks, especially in the lower school. This can help to form essential learning relationships early in a child's secondary career and enable more creative teaching and learning, less bound by hourly bells and subject divisions. Further, education also needs to focus on how to build relationships and fragile self-esteem, since colleges often recruit students who have struggled in the school system and some institutions and tutors are very aware of this (NRDC, 2005)

Activity 6.4

From your reading, your own experience and discussions with others can you identify ways in which you could support the emotional aspects of learning and development either with children, parents or colleagues?

Conclusion

It is reassuring to see an increased understanding of affective issues in education in the United Kingdom, both in the curriculum and in teacher professional development.

Neuroscience has reinforced the understandings from psychology and has established its significance in learning and interaction. Educational research has established that some contexts support profound empathy (which supports learning) better than others. The next leap in understanding to be made is in tackling the problems of the hidden curriculum of contexts and ratios and the fragmented curriculum and normative assessment. Interaction and exchange with parents is increasing and Sure Start aims to begin this process at an early age. Support for parents struggling with their own and their children's problems is vital in all areas such as education, employment, health and social services.

Emotional capital is a term which describes what we all need to build and maintain in terms of our emotional development. Emotional strength can dissipate when traumatic or compounding life events from birth to the grave, lower confidence and esteem. For those whose sense of self has been battered or denied from an early age, their need for positive, trusting human relationships is even greater. This is hard to find in large classes, where teachers and senior managers are focused on a wealth of content, skills and 'activities' to enhance performance, rather than finding time to listen to the needs and wants of their children. How we feel about our learning affects how and what we learn and allowing time and space for profound empathy to emerge in human relationships may well hold the secret for fantastic leaps in future learning and development.

Summary

- emotion is significant in human development
- being aware of affect in education is important
- types of empathy in teaching and learning
- constraints on empathy in the education system; classroom and school levels
- ways to address emotional issues in today's schools
- ideas for best practice at classroom and school levels

References

Aspy, D (1972) *Towards a Technology for Humanising Education*. Champaign, Illinois: Illinois Research Press

Best, R (2003) 'Struggling with the spiritual in education', *Tenth International Conference Education Spirituality and the Whole Child Conference,* London: University of Surrey Roehampton

Brandes, D and Ginnis, P (1990) *The Student-Centred School*. London: Blackwell

Brown, L (ed.) (1993) *The New Oxford Shorter Dictionary*. USA: Oxford University Press

Bowlby, J (1951) *Child Care and the Growth of Love*. Harmondsworth: Penguin

Cooper, B (2002) 'Teachers as moral models? The role of empathy in teacher/pupil relationships', PhD thesis: Leeds Metropolitan University

Cooper, B (2004) 'Empathy, interaction and caring; teachers' roles in a constrained environment', *Pastoral Care in Education,* 22(3)

Cooper, B (2007) 'The significance of affect in multi-modal communication: lessons for on-line learning', *The International Journal of Interactive Technology and Smart Education, Special issue, in press*

Cooper, B and Brna, P (2003) 'The significance of affective issues in successful learning with ICT for year one and two pupils and their teachers: the final outcomes of the ICT and Whole child project', British Educational Research Association Conference, Edinburgh: Herriot-Watt University

Damasio, A (1994) *Descartes' Error.* London: Macmillan

Damasio, A (1999) *The Feeling of What Happens: Body, Emotion and the Making of Consciousness.* London: Vintage

Darciaz, D (2007) 'Triune ethics theory a neurobiologically-based moral psychology', Annual Conference of the Association of Moral Education, New York, November

DfES (2003) 'Excellence and enjoyment – a strategy for primary schools', London; DFES

Fischer, E (1973) *Marx in His Own Words.* Middlesex: Penguin

Francescato, D (1998) 'Affective education and teacher training in Italy', in Lang, P, Katz, Y and Menezes, I (eds), *Affective Education.* London: Cassell

Goleman, D (1995) *Emotional Intelligence.* London: Bloomsbury

Hargreaves, D H (1972) *The Challenge for the Comprehensive School, Culture, Curriculum and Community.* London: Routledge and Kegan Paul

Hay, D (1997) 'Spiritual education and values', *Education, Spirituality and the Whole Child Conference,* Roehampton Institute, May

HMSO (2003) *Every Child Matters* (green paper), London: TSO

Hoban, G F (2002) 'Teacher learning for educational change', Buckingham: OUP

Hume, D (1739) 'A treatise of human nature', in Honderich, T. (ed.), (1995) *Oxford Companion to Philosophy.* Oxford: Oxford University Press

Kozeki, B and Berghammer, R (1992) 'The role of empathy in the motivational structure of school children', *Personality and Individual Difference,* 13(2)

Kyriacou, C (1986) *Effective Teaching in Schools.* Hemel Hempstead: Simon and Schuster

Leal, M R (2002) 'The caring relationship', *Ninth Annual International Conference Education Spirituality and the Whole Child,* London: Roehampton, June

Maclean Hospital (2001) www.mclean.harvard.edu/PublicAffairs/20001214_child_abuse.htm

Macmurray, J (1935) *Reason and Emotion.* London: Faber and Faber

McCarthy, K (2000) 'Learning by heart: the role of emotional education in raising school achievement and promoting the caring community', in Best, R (ed.) *Education for Spiritual, Moral, Social and Cultural Development,* London: Continuum

Marx, K and Engels, F (1888) *Manifesto of the Communist Party.* Moscow: originally Progress Publishers

Noddings, N (1986) *Caring – a Feminine Approach to Ethics and Moral Education* USA: University of California Press

NRDC (2005) 'Embedded teaching and learning of adult literacy, numeracy and ESOL', London: NRDC

Pike, G and Selby, D (1988) *Global Teacher, Global Learner.* London: Hodder and Stoughton (with York University)

Priestley, J (2000) 'Curriculum and Kierkegaard: towards creating a paradigm for discerning the spiritual dimension of education', in Best, R (ed.) *Education for Spiritual, Moral, Social and Cultural Development,* London: Continuum

Rogers, C R (1975) 'Empathic: an unappreciated way of being', *The Counselling Psychologist,* 5(2), 2

Sacks, O (1985) *The Man who Mistook his Wife for a Hat.* London: Picador

Sacks, O (1996) *The Island of the Colour Blind.* London: Picador

Schantz, C U (1975) 'Empathy in relation to social cognitive development', *The Counselling Psychologist,* 5(2), 18

Vygotsky, L S (1976) *Mind in Society.* London and Massachusetts: Harvard University Press

Vygotsky, L S (1986) *Thought and Language.* Translation newly revised by Alex Kozulin Cambridge, MA: MIT Press

Watson, B and Ashton, E (1995) *Education, Assumptions and Values.* London: David Fulton

Watt, D F (2000) 'Emotion and consciousness: implications of affective neurosciences for extended reticular thalamic activating system theories of consciousness'. Available at: www.phil.vt.edu/ASSC/watt/default.htm.

Winkley, D (1996) 'Towards the human school – principles and practice', Conference Paper *Beyond Market Forces – Creating the Human School,* Birmingham: West Hill College, February

Further reading

Damasio, A (1999) *The Feeling of What Happens: Body, Emotion and the Making of Consciousness.* London: Vintage

Damasio, A (2003) *Looking for Spinoza: Joy Sorrow and the Feeling Brain.* London: Heinemann

Goleman, D (1995) *Emotional Intelligence.* London: Bloomsbury

Kyriacou, C (1986) *Effective Teaching in Schools.* Hemel Hempstead: Simon and Schuster

Macgilchrist, B, Myers, K and Reed, J (2004) *The Intelligent School.* London: Sage

Useful websites

www.antidote.org.uk/ – Antidote works with schools to help shape learning environments where everyone is motivated and able to participate.

www.seal.org.uk – Society for Effective Affective Learning (SEAL). SEAL promotes learning approaches which embrace body, emotions, mind and spirit to enable people to develop their full potential.

www.jennymosley.demon.co.uk – The Whole School Quality Circle Time Mode. Has a commitment to building children's sense of self-worth and helping them to care more about the feelings of those around them.

www.childpsychotherapytrust.org.uk – The Child Psychotherapy Trust. Works to promote understanding of children's emotional health and to increase access to psychotherapy services for young people in need.

www.surestart.gov.ac.uk – Sure Start is a government programme which seeks to link all the agencies connected with early child development and learning to ensure children have the best start in life.

Useful internet search terms

affective issues in learning

emotion and learning

empathy and learning

emotional intelligence in teaching and learning

personalized learning

self-esteem and learning

emotional and behavioural needs

special educational needs and self-esteem

emotion and moral development

Part II
Contexts for Education

Breaking Barriers to Learning 7

Pat Hughes

Chapter Outline

Introduction

Most people when asked about who works in school would probably start off with teachers. Then if there remained a pregnant silence would move on to other school-based workers such as site managers, cleaners and administrators. When children are asked this, they generally include themselves very early on. It is as if we retain a memory of the old Victorian and Edwardian photographs of classrooms with a teacher, pupils and perhaps the odd pupil monitor. Today's schools are staffed very differently and the flexibility of workforce reform has meant that there is an increased recognition that schools are staffed to support children's learning and everyone has a key role.

The expression 'barriers to learning' comes from the initial documentation related to the creation, training and employment of school-based learning mentors (Hughes in Campbell and Fairbairn, 2005).

Activity 7.1 Identifying Staff Working in Schools Who Are Directly Involved in Breaking Barriers to Learning

When you next visit a school, look carefully for adults working both inside and outside classrooms and nurseries. Identify how their role improves children's learning. It is useful to remember that the title of posts varies from school to school and often from one local authority to another. One useful way of finding out the titles of many (but not all) of those working in a particular school is via the school prospectus. Most schools have these on their own websites.

Case Study 7.1 A School Journey

My tour of a local primary school starts before I arrive. Standing on the playground, talking to a parent is Adam the Learning Mentor. Later we will look at his role more closely. Again it is useful to remember at this stage that the names, roles, pay of many of adult workers in school vary from school to school and from one local authority to another.

I enter the school pushing the door bell to check me into the building. Already, the safety of all those working within the building has been under scrutiny. Twenty years ago, I could just walk straight into any school, through any door. Now only one door is open. Once in, I sign a book to say who I am, what time I have arrived, my car number, who I am employed by, whom I am visiting and later my exit time. This also provides some security for me should anything happen to the building. It is these very small details, which have increased over time, which are part of creating a secure building for all those working inside and outside.

The small office is staffed by a secretary and two administrative assistants. Also sitting there at 8:45 a.m. is the site manager and the head teacher. Both these have been in school since 6:45 a.m. and are now having a well deserved cup of tea. A teaching assistant is using the photocopier.

I then turn left into the school and walk down a small set of steps, which were altered some years ago to accommodate children, staff and visitors with mobility issues. Turning into the first room, I met with the parent mentor, three parents and one eight-month-old baby. We chat briefly about the work they are doing and I move down the corridor to meet with a teacher with whom I used to work. In the classroom, the children are beginning to settle and she has three other adults with her. One is a teaching assistant (TA) and the other a special needs assistant (SNA). Neither will be in the same classroom all day. The third adult is a student-teacher undertaking a placement. On another day in this classroom, a trainee teaching assistant works in the room. All four adults have children's learning as a priority and the class teacher has to organize her team to ensure that maximum learning takes place.

I then come out of this classroom and go upstairs to my reason for visiting. Today, I am a student taking a European Computer Driving License. The class is run by a further education lecturer from the local community college. The other students are either parents or people working in the school. We are all doing different courses and are at different stages and the provision is part of the local authorities programme called Family and Community Education (FACE). Its aim is to skill up members of the community, to give them confidence as well as skills to improve their and their children's life chance.

As I leave the school, I meet with the local safety inspector who is running a cycling award course on the playground for the Y5 children.

All these people are school-based because it is seen that their work has relevance to children's learning. This has been made clearer under the Every Child Matters Agenda, although at least two of those I met on my tour would not be under the remit of the Integrated Children's Services department of the Local Authority.

Factors influencing barriers to learning

This section identifies how particular branches of the social sciences have identified specific factors which influence an individual's life chances. The growth in the number of staff employed directly by schools, or by other agencies to work in schools is directly related to a deeper awareness of how children learn. And linked closely to this is the growth in understanding of what may form barriers to learning and strategies to overcome these barriers. This overview of the potential research field may look alarming. It can also look rather fatalistic when we start examining it at the big picture level. This starts by recognizing that there are global as well as national, local and individual reasons why some pupils many have more challenges in learning within schools (Figure 7.1). Indeed global factors influence our school curriculum as our schools contain an increasing number of pupils who have – or have not been – schooled elsewhere (Table 7.1). Migration has been a continual part of global history.

Whether they can be recognized or not, these influences have important implications for children's learning and part of the Training and Development Agency (TDA) drive to improve the educational standards of those working in schools has been to encourage subject knowledge which informs strategies to breakdown barriers to learning.

Acitivity 7.2

Maslow's basic hierarchy of needs (2000) provides a seminal understanding of some of the key barriers to learning found in many schools today (Figure 7.2).

Use the latest DCSF publication for the 'Common Core of Skills and Knowledge for the Children's Workforce' and identify which particular skills and strategies might be used to support barriers of learning related to physical, safety and belongingness needs. For example, the provision of a breakfast at school can support a basic physiological need and the opportunity to chat one to one with an adult before school can support a safety need.

Decide how these might conflict with the traditional role of the teacher to ensure that all children and young people have access to a broad and balanced National Curriculum? For example, in some areas many children have very basic needs which are not met outside school. This means that children and young people enter school with learning needs that are not going to be met by the formal curriculum. How might their response show itself in relation to this conflict with the working environment of the classroom or learning centre?

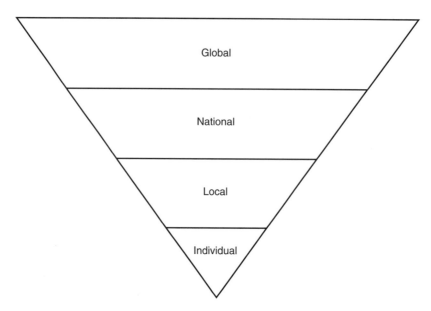

Figure 7.1 Migration.

Table 7.1 Relevant influences on pupils in today's schools

Research area	Relevant influences on pupils in today's schools
Historical	Tradition of schooling in this country; oral history of schooling within a child's family; their own experience of schooling.
Sociological	Life-chances; labelling; distinct groups, communities and family patterns identified as 'problematic'. These include race, gender, class, faith, special need.
Psychological	Learning theories; developmental and personal psychology; social psychology, including the social construction of childhood.
Economic	Poverty – in a community and/or family; built-in limits on central/local government and family funding.
Political	Political ideologies related to education resulting in legislation and guidelines (local and national) covering nearly all of school provision; rights of the individual; role of the state; inspection procedures – the national Ofsted report for 2002 identified under performance in disproportional numbers in minority ethnic and faith groups; travellers, asylum seekers and refugees; pupils with English as an additional language (EAL); pupils with special needs (SEN); looked after children'; gifted and talented; other children such as sick children, young carers, families under stress, pregnant girls, teenage mothers; disaffected and excluded pupils.
Geographical	Demographic factors; economic, social, political and regional factors; international relations.
Legal	International, European and national rights of the child; statutory obligations related to attendance, behaviour towards children etc.
Educational	Educational policy, technology, teaching methods, training of teachers and other educators including all of the above.

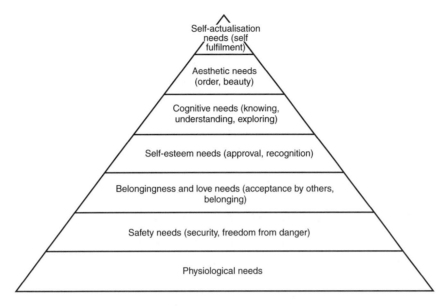

Figure 7.2 Maslow's basic hierarchy of needs.

Who's who in schools?

1. Allied Professionals employed by the school

Activity 7.3

There were many other workers in school on my tour day. Write down as many people as you can think of who you might meet on a tour around a school. You might decide to identify some allied professional who are generic to all schools as well as those whom you might find only in specific schools, for example, in secondary schools.

Your list may include the welfare staff, who supervise the children at lunch time and who have had several courses on outdoor play, the cook and catering staff who had been involved with courses on healthy eating and hygiene, voluntary workers, specialist support staff, professionals from other public services, professionals from charities and local faith workers. A tour round a secondary school is more complex with many other allied professionals who help to break down barriers to learning. These may include counsellors, integrated services co-ordinator, librarians, technicians and subject specialists who are not trained teachers.

These adults are often given the generic title of paraprofessionals, although the term allied professionals is also used as being more generous about the type of work they do (Hughes, 2008). Rates of pay and conditions of service vary considerably. Often there are surprising differences between two workers who appear to be doing much the same work in the same school.

Allied Educational Professionals employed by the school may:

- work semi-autonomously with pupils throughout the day and report to a line manager, either within or outside the school
- give generic learning support in classes or learning units with work or assessment tasks prepared by the class or subject teacher
- work with a child identified with special learning needs
- work or manage a unit or centre within the school
- work in more than one role, for example, a teaching assistant in the morning and a learning mentor in the afternoon.
- have variable training and qualifications

2. Volunteers – linked to one or two schools

There are also, particularly in primary schools, unpaid volunteers. Some may spend whole days in school, others just a couple of hours a week. These include

- parents and carers and other relatives
- community workers
- partnership workers
- governors
- student teachers
- work experience/trainees
- former teachers
- charity workers, e.g., Volunteer Reading Help (VRH)

All schools must have a Governing Body and their constituency is laid down by law. Governors are responsible for taking part in performance management for the head teacher, interviewing potential staff, sitting on appeals panels for both staff and pupils, taking part in policy formation and many other areas of school life. As with most volunteer roles, a good school governor can spend a massive amount of time on this sort of activity as well as working as a volunteer in classrooms, on residential courses, outdoor pursuits and so on.

3. Educational support workers – not employed by the school, but whose services may be paid from the school budget

There are a range of other workers, not employed by the school directly, but whose work can be closely linked to improving and enhancing children and young people's learning (Table 7.2). These include:

- pupil attendance and education welfare
- primary care trust workers such as school nurses
- special needs integrated support

Table 7.2 External providers – employed by public and private agencies

Local authority (integrated services, police, leisure, libraries etc.)	Emergency duty team	Youth offending team
Children's Family Court Advisory and Support Service (CAFCASS)	Primary Care Trust (PCT)	Child and Adolescent Mental Health Services (CAMHS)
Substance misuse	Anti-smoking	NSPCC
Child line	Barnardos	Children's society
Before and after school clubs	Local authority initiatives linked to specific strategies such as literacy, numeracy and citizenship	Play and holiday schemes
Theatre in education	Author/artist in residence schemes	Etc.

- behaviour support
- ethnic minority support
- connexions
- integrated children's services manager

Training

The government is determined, quite rightly, to try and ensure that all those working in schools have the qualifications and skills to do so. For allied professionals employed by the school these are still very variable and can be school based, cluster based, local authority, further education or higher education based; nationally based – including online provision – self-determined professional development and life experienced based. Many allied professionals have qualifications prior to their employment by a particular school. An increasing number of Higher Learning Teaching Assistants (HLTA), TAs and Special Teaching Assistants (STA), for example, have degrees or are studying for a degree.

Not only does training vary but so does salary. Some allied professionals are on yearly full pay, like teachers; many are paid 'pro-rata'. Pro-rata means that they only get paid for term times and this can cut their yearly pay by as much as a third. Sometimes pay may be based on qualifications and specialist skills held; sometimes on recommended national rates. Some may be school based, often on informal negotiation and some are negotiated at local level via trade unions.

The Common Core of Knowledge and Skills initially published by the DfES (2005), identified six areas of skills and knowledge required for those working with children. It was intended to consolidate and extend the existing qualifications provision and to make it more easily recognized and accessible nationally. It will take many years to see how successful and effective this has been in breaking barriers to learning in our schools.

- effective communication and engagement with children, young people and families
- child and young person development
- safeguarding and promoting the welfare of the child
- supporting transitions
- multi-agency working
- sharing information

A visit to the qualifications section of the Children's Workforce Development Council (CWDC) provides a link to the various qualifications available for those working with children. These appear quite detailed but much will depend on the nature of the training, both on and offsite. Detailed central government input can result in some low-level briefing training, with few opportunities for discussion, visits to other placements and opportunities to develop questioning and critique skills on current practice. Sadly, many of the case studies available online or in publications rarely are 'warts and all' accounts (Chiosso in Jones et al., 2008) and this makes it extremely difficult to use them for effective learning. The 'sanitised format' is usually policy focused and written to demonstrate how well government guidance works. Real life is rarely so easy and also complicated by many of the facts identified in the research areas outlined above.

The training of external providers is even more variable. Clearly there are specific professional training qualifications which they require; for example school nurses come from a nursing and social work background. Professional courses are already incorporating aspects of integrated training within their courses and looking carefully at new developments across agencies as well as within their own agency. However, there are issues of knowledge and skills overload as staff look to professional confidence in their own speciality as well as awareness of what else is developing within the integrated children's agenda.

Exemplars of educational allied professionals

The learning mentor

Twelve years ago it would have been rare to find learning mentors in the English Education System or indeed many of the other allied professionals found now, whose brief it was to 'break down barriers to learning.' The history of their introduction and success in schools provides a useful rationale for many of the role definitions we now find assigned to allied professionals. For this reason, a brief look at their development provides a useful practical and theoretical base for this chapter.

Background

Learning mentors came out of one strand of the Department for Education and Skills (DfES) Excellence in Cities (EiC) programme. This expanding initiative was introduced in March

1999 to tackle 'specific problems facing children in our cities. Through a combination of initiatives, it (EiC) aims to raise the aspirations and achievements of pupils and to tackle disaffection, social exclusion, truancy and indiscipline and improve parents' confidence in cities'. (Hughes, 2005, 2008).

The EiC initiative used good practice projects from within the United Kingdom, but also imported ideas from the United States (e.g. magnet schools). The programme was largely met with enthusiasm by the schools in these areas, which saw it as a recognition that more than words were needed to raise aspirations and hope for pupils in their schools. Since then the initiative has expanded across most schools in the country and has been subject to two excellent National Training Programmes. The programmes provide mentors with a formal qualification.

The current DfES website on learning mentors defines learning mentors as:

- salaried staff who work with school and college students and pupils to help them address barriers to learning
- a bridge across academic and pastoral support roles with the aim of ensuring that individual pupils and students engage more effectively in learning and achieve appropriately
- a key ingredient in many school and college approaches to improvement the achievement levels of pupils and students.

The overall purpose of their role is to promote effective participation, enhance individual learning, raise aspirations and achieve their potential (Table 7.3).

This involves mentors having a good knowledge as well as skills base. Particular aspects of this are useful to see in relation to other allied professionals whose role it is to raise achievement in schools. Below are just a few of the tasks they undertake to enhance pupils' learning.

Activity 7.4

Use Maslow's hierarchy of basic needs to identify which specific basic needs may be met by some of these strategies. Can you identify some potential conflicts in empowering school students to have a voice in their community/school?

The teaching assistant

Since the late 1990s, there has been a massive increase in the number of support workers in classrooms. In this section, the focus is the growth and changing role of teaching assistants while being aware that other workers in the classroom may have a different name but be doing much the same role. They are all working to break down barriers to learning.

Table 7.3 Possible tasks undertaken by primary learning mentors

Strategy	Rationale
1. Monitor and improve attendance – this involves developing whole school and individual strategies to encourage reluctant attenders to come into school.	Ensure students build a habit of attending school and reinforce to both carers and pupils that this is important. Ofsted inspections see attendance as a crucial issue and government legislation distinguishes between authorized and unauthorized absence.
2. Establish one-to-one mentoring and other supportive relationships with children and young people.	To support individual pupils who are failing to learn effectively for a variety of reasons. Mentors draw on their knowledge and skills to provide effective strategies to enable pupils to feel more 'relaxed and alert' about coming to school and being confident about learning. They may run specific activities to help pupils with issues such as anger management, emotional development and anti-stress.
3. Support the PSHE curriculum within schools – often through individual work, but also via direct teaching with whole classes e.g. circle time.	Mentoring training involves drawing on new insights into PSHE. They are often the only ones in schools who receive regular training on these issues and their knowledge of individual pupils can help inform other integrated children's and young people's services such as health and social care.
4. Establishment of schools' councils and parliaments.	Empowering students to feel that they have a voice in their community, providing practical exemplars of citizenship, identifying key issues about the inner workings of the school which may be missed by adults e.g. bullying.

The number of TAs in English schools rose from 60,000 in 1997 to more than 153,000 at the time of writing. They are all expected to have or to take some basic related qualifications, if they do not already have some.

- one out of ten has completed training in order to become a HLTA
- a survey by the Institute of Education in London shows that one in eight of TAs is educated to degree level or above.

But

- one in five has no permanent contract and
- only one in seven was paid during school holidays

And

- ninety eight per cent of all TAs are women.

The sharp growth in the number of TAs since 1997 can be linked to three different factors: the inclusion of SEN pupils into main stream schools; the introduction of National Literacy and Numeracy strategies which required additional adult support in primary schools and technological advances. During this time, both training and responsibility for TAs developed. *Raising standards and tackling workload* (DfES, 2003) was linked to teacher work load, but impacted significantly on changes in the roles and responsibilities of TAs. Table 7.4 lists possible tasks undertaken by TAs in primary schools.

The status – if not the pay – of TAs was raised when the Teaching Training Agency (TTA) became the Training and Development Agency (TDA) and was charged with training responsibility for all those working in schools. Their roles are very directly related to breaking down barriers to learning for individual pupils, and often providing non-contact or supply cover for teachers. It can be argued that this provides continuity and is more effective than employing supply teachers. However, it can also be argued, mostly notably by the National Union of Teachers (NUT), who were not a party to this agreement, that this extension of the role can be a cheap way of fulfilling the government's promise to decrease teacher workload.

The table shows how pervasive the role of the TA is. Some of it is administrative, some teaching, some pastoral. It will vary from school to school, as do the names for those performing the role.

Parent/carer mentors

Educating or 're-educating' parents and carers has been seen by several governments over many decades to be one of the ways in which children's learning, behaviour, sense of citizenship and so on can be improved. It has been school based and area based. A considerable slice of the adult education budget in many authorities has been linked with the second aspect of parent mentoring, namely skilling up parents to produce the sort of citizens who know their responsibilities. At the time of writing 'parenting' is receiving a good deal of attention and parenting officers are being appointed and courses created. These may be called parenting courses, but they are often hid under other names such as Family Learning. There are mixed views about parenting courses; including views on what good parenting is. Poverty does not make a poor parent, nor does wealth make a good one so why does the concentration on parenting always seem to focus on those living in deprived areas?

Table 7.4 Possible tasks undertaken by TAs in primary schools

Provide specialist support for literacy, numeracy, ICT	Run booster classes	Be early years managers
Nurture group leaders	Behaviour support specialists	SEN specialists
Cover supervisors	TA manager	Travellers pupil specialist
EAL support	Counsellors	Pastoral year heads
Invigilators and markers for SATs	Resource administrators	Parental liaison administrators

Note: Anything else created uniquely to suit the school's needs and TA expertise.

Paid parent mentors tend to be found in economically disadvantaged areas, where central government targets parents and carers to support their own children's learning and development. They also provide opportunities for parents/carers to develop new skills and qualifications for themselves.

In the School Journey above, the parent mentor was employed in a local authority where there was a recently created Family Learning service. This aimed to provide range of courses and activities that

- helped parents/carers engage with and support their children's learning and development
- provided opportunities for parents/carers to develop new skills, gain qualifications
- supported children's learning

The service acknowledged that because learning was a whole family, intergenerational process there was more than one way of working than a set of specific programmes. The parent mentor programme is therefore just a very small part of a much wider initiative. The New Deal for Communities provides fund for parent mentors. The aim is to support and engage parents and the local community, promote family learning and parental partnership, promote opportunities for parents to take part in adult education and provide a range of other support, for example, credit union, health awareness, volunteering. Funding for these and other projects is often an issue and the long-term survival of courses, child support and so on linked to such funding is always at risk.

Looking at Research

Chiosso in Jones et al. (2008) provides a useful introduction to critiquing such projects when written up as case studies. She herself looked at a playground project over several years. Fund bidding was a key element in the success or not of initiatives over the whole period and of course continues to be. It is very easy to see this in any project in your local area, which is dependent on bidding for a substantial amount of its running cost.

The educational social worker

Central Area Support Team (CAST) is a multi-agency team working in an extremely economically deprived Local Authority as part of the Integrated Children's Service.

Case Study 7.2

A dishevelled, bare foot mother rushed past me to the head's room. This mother's difficulties were well known to the school. She managed to cope by herself with three young children on benefits for so long and then broke down. She had a substance misuse problem and mixed this with medication from her GP.

Two hours later, the educational social worker had been called in and a partial 'solution' drawn up. The mother was committed and the children would by the end of the school day be taken into care.

No-one pretends this is ideal, but the speed at which the school was able to get in the Educational Social Worker (EWO) was impressive and the area knowledge the worker had meant that the solution could be found quickly. Figure 7.3 shows how schools in this particular authority are able to access support from EWOs for young people 'whose needs are not critical'; although in this case the need had been critical and identified directly by the school.

The ESW was part of a team based about two miles from the school. This team covered an educational psychologist, educational social work, sensory impairment and specialist teachers for learning, access and inclusion (behaviour). Employment was via former Local Authority health, social care and education departments, now part of an Integrated Children's Services programme. Also involved as an employer is the local Primary Care Trust. In addition the base included a school for children with moderate learning difficulties which also acted as a part-time school for some main-stream learners with reading difficulties, autistic spectrum disorders and emotional health and well-being issues. CAST also acted as a centre for Portage, Sure Start, School Improvement, School Attendance, Health Visitors, School Nurses, Speech and Language Therapy, Social Services, CAMHS and the Child Development team. This helps develop efficient communication systems between

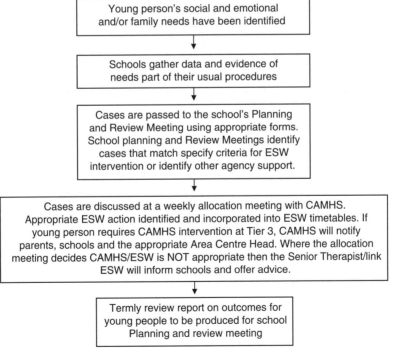

Figure 7.3 Tier 2 process for schools to access support from ESW for young people whose needs are not critical.

schools and services. A usefully sized training room with coffee and tea making facilities helps to encourage meetings between different agencies. The area site is still in its early days and it will be interesting to follow its progress and development over several years in terms of improved provision for children and young people in the area.

Conclusion

The school workforce has changed considerably over the last few years and provides a useful example of how government philosophy and politics influence the study and practice of compulsory education. In particular the role of the teacher, who now becomes a team leader, and by default a member of a multi-agency service for all children.

Summary

This chapter has explored

- the range of staff who work in schools
- roles and training of these different workers

References

Chiosso, R (2008) 'The swings and roundabouts of community development', in Jones et al. (2008) *Childhood: Services and Provision for Children*. London: Pearson

DfES (2003) 'Raising standards and tackling workload', Nottingham: DfES

DfES (2005) 'Common core of skills and knowledge for the children's workforce', Nottingham: DfES

Fairbairn, G and Campbell, A (2005) 'Working with support in the classroom', London: Chapman

Hughes, P (2005) 'Learning mentors in primary classrooms and schools', chapter 4 in Campbell, A and Fairbairn, G (eds), *Working with Support in the Classroom*. London: Chapman

Hughes, P (2008) *Principles of Primary Education*. London: Routledge

Jones, P, Moss, D, Tomlinson, P and Welch, S (2008) *Childhood: Services and Provision for Children*. London: Pearson

Information for TAs and other support staff is available on the dedicated area of TeacherNet. www.teachernet.gov.uk/wholeschool/supportstaff/

Further reading

Barron, I, Holmes, R and MacLure, M (2008) 'Primary schools and other agencies', in *Primary Review*. Cambridge: Cambridge University

Burgess, H (2008) 'Primary workforce, management & reform', in *Primary Review*. Cambridge: Cambridge University

Cheshire NUT (2006) 'Teachers and teaching assistants: working together: a training pack for schools and colleges.' secretary@cheshire.nut.org.uk

Griffiths, T, Stead, D and Hughes, P (2006) 'Every child matters', in *Earth and Beyond*. This is a DVD which contains a 15-minute science lesson with a voice-over looking at implications for the ECM agenda. The same lesson is examined from a primary science perspective and from a class management perspective. Available from Di. Stead at Liverpool Hope University

Useful websites

www.primaryreview.org.uk – This website gives details of the UK government's review of primary education.

www.dfes.gov.uk/publications/childrensplan/ – This website has the latest version of UK government document such as the Children's Plan. Other publications can also be found from the home page.

www.everychildmatters.gov.uk – This website will lead you to the range of people who work in schools and Children's Centres.

Useful internet search terms

barriers to learning

Maslow

school governors

connexions

educational support workers

learning mentors

teaching assistants

Safeguarding Children and Adults in Educational Settings

Gary Walker

Introduction

This chapter will focus on the role of schools and further education colleges, and of individual staff within them, in safeguarding children and adults in England. Schools are in the unique position among the agencies involved with children of being accessed by large numbers of children, and of having intensive day-to-day contact with them. This means that they know the children and young people well, and are aware of wider family circumstances, sometimes educating two or more generations. The chapter has two distinct sections. In the first, current systems and guidance on the role of schools and responsibilities of individual staff members in safeguarding children are explained. The second section considers the role of schools and colleges in safeguarding adults (i.e. anyone over the age of 17) who attend schools and colleges. The chapter will not cover in any depth the role of schools in vetting and recruiting staff.

Safeguarding children in schools and colleges

What do we mean by safeguarding?

The government's Every Child Matters programme (DfES, 2003) promotes a positive and preventative approach whereby agencies are expected to intervene early when there are concerns for a child's welfare. To reflect this, the terms 'safeguarding children' and 'promoting their welfare' replaced the previous narrower term 'child protection'. The national guidance Working Together to Safeguard Children (DfES, 2006a) states that safeguarding children and promoting their welfare means

- protecting children from maltreatment
- preventing impairment of children's health or development
- ensuring that children grow up in circumstances consistent with the provision of safe and effective care
- professionals enabling children to have optimum life chances and to enter adulthood successfully

What was previously called 'child protection' is now seen as a sub-set of safeguarding and promoting the welfare of children. The guidance goes on to say that children need protecting when they are suffering, or likely to suffer, significant harm and the harm is attributable to a lack of adequate parental care or control. There are no absolute criteria for judging what 'significant' harm is, but in doing so, professionals should consider the severity of any ill-treatment, and the degree, extent, duration and frequency of harm.

Following on from this, four categories of abuse are used, the full definitions of which are provided within the government guidance (DfES, 2006a):

- physical abuse
- sexual abuse
- emotional abuse
- neglect

How many children need safeguarding?

National guidance on the assessment of children and their families (DH, DfEE and HO, 2000) refers to 'vulnerable children' making up approximately one third of all children, which in England amounts to approximately four million children. The definition of 'vulnerable children' used here refers to 'those disadvantaged children who would benefit from extra help from public agencies in order to make the best of their life chances' (ibid.: 2).

Of the various subsets of these vulnerable children, this chapter focuses on those in need of protection. There are around 26,000 children on the child protection register in

England at any one time. However, these are merely the children the authorities know about, and as such represent the tip of an iceberg. A seminal report (National Commission of Inquiry into the Prevention of Child Abuse, 1996) based on 10,000 contributions from a range of professionals, members of the public, children and leading experts in the field found that abuse appears to be significantly under-reported, such that the real figures might be thus:

Children suffering severe physical punishment	150,000
Children experiencing sexual exploitation	100,000
Children living in low-warmth, high-criticism environments (Emotional abuse)	350,000
Children being bullied at school at least once a week	450,000
Children living with domestic violence	250,000

Clearly although there may be some double counting here, in that the same child may be experiencing harm under more than one category, these figures put the potential number of children experiencing serious harm at 1.3 million, or one in ten.

This may seem alarming, yet similar figures have been found in further studies. Cawson et al. (2000) found that 21 per cent of girls and 11 per cent of boys had experienced child sexual abuse. Figures from the Department of Health (DH, 2002) indicate that at least 750,000 children witness domestic violence each year. This equates to approximately 1 child in 17. The precise figures can be argued over; however the general point is that children do get harmed in various ways, and that staff working in schools need to be aware of this, and furthermore that boys and girls from all social classes, ethnic or religious backgrounds are potentially at risk.

Activity 8.1

The evidence suggests that each year significant numbers of children are abused and harmed either directly or indirectly by adults.

What reasons can you think of for this?

You might consider the position of children in society – their relative lack of power and rights – and what Hanvey (2003) calls 'the deep ambiguity about children, seeing them as angels or villains' (2003: 1) coupled with a 'lack of collective and individual responsibility for the safety of vulnerable children within communities' (ibid.). You might also want to consider how most of the legislation regarding children emphasizes that children are effectively the private property of parents, and that others should only interfere with parenting if the child is at risk.

National guidance for schools and colleges on safeguarding children

The key guidance document here is entitled 'Safeguarding Children and Safer Recruitment in Education' (DfES, 2006b). This covers the school sector (local authority and private primary, secondary and special schools and pupil referral units, attended by excluded pupils), the responsibility of local authorities and the Further Education sector (colleges that provide education for students under the age of 18). Of the three bodies to whom this guidance is aimed – schools, colleges and local authorities – the focus will be on the role of schools and colleges and the term 'schools' will be used to cover both.

Responsibilities of schools and colleges

Technically, it is the responsibility of the governing bodies of schools to ensure that each establishment has effective safeguarding children procedures, and that it adheres to them. Governing bodies should have no involvement with, or oversight of, individual cases; rather they take a strategic lead in ensuring compliance with the guidance.

The role of head teachers in safeguarding children

Head teachers should ensure that the school's child protection policy and procedures are fully implemented. They should commit sufficient resources and time to allow staff to fulfil their responsibilities, including attendance at meetings, or contributing to multi-agency assessments. They should ensure that all staff feel able to raise concerns about poor or unsafe practice, and where this happens, to respond appropriately.

Child protection policy

Schools should have a child protection policy in place. This policy should be in line with local or national guidance, and should be made available to parents upon request. Local authorities provide more detailed guidance to schools on what should be included in a policy. Generally speaking, it should detail how the school, and every individual within it, will fulfil safeguarding children responsibilities. An example of a school child protection policy is available on the Teachernet website (see 'Useful websites' at the end of this chapter). Alternatively, 'education child protection team' or 'education safeguarding children team' within local authorities can be contacted for further information.

A designated officer for child protection

Schools should have in place at least one senior member of staff to take lead responsibility for child protection. The national guidance goes onto specify that the designated person should lead the co-ordination of child protection activity within the school, provide advice and support to staff, and liaise with the local authority and work with other agencies. Furthermore, although, in schools, they need not be a teacher, they 'must have the status and authority within the school management structure to carry out the duties of the post . . . including committing resources to child protection matters, and where appropriate directing other staff' (DfES, 2006b: 14).

Training for staff

The designated person for child protection should undertake initial training for their role, and refresher training every two years. Furthermore, all school staff, including the head teacher, should have child protection training which is refreshed at least every three years. The local authority has the responsibility to ensure that schools comply with this, and they usually not only provide or broker appropriate training, but monitor attendance at such training. This training typically includes topics such as recognizing possible signs of harm, dealing with a direct disclosure of abuse from a child, appropriate monitoring and recording of concerns about children, and the school's role in referring concerns on to, and subsequent liaison with, other agencies. As an alternative to the local authority, schools can also access training via a range of organizations such as the National Society for the Prevention of Cruelty to Children (NSPCC) who provide both face-to-face and distance training packages (see 'Useful websites' at the end of this chapter for more details).

Looking at Research 8.1

A survey of 327 schools in England found that all but one had a designated teacher for child protection, and 94 per cent had a child protection policy. However, 88 per cent had concerns that not all teachers would be able to recognize signs of abuse, and just under two-thirds of schools reported some degree of uncertainty about when to contact social services in relation to a child protection concern. For 92 per cent of the schools, there was some concern about how to maintain relationships with parents when the schools were involved in child protection cases, and 88 per cent of schools reported having some concerns about how they could best support children when they disclose abuse to staff (Baginsky, 2000).

Liaison with other agencies

Within safeguarding children work, schools have a clear responsibility to work closely with other agencies where necessary. This includes making direct referrals to children's social care services where necessary and appropriate, and subsequently working with them and other agencies which may become involved, such as the police or health professionals. This liaison may involve telephone conversations and face-to-face meetings. The designated person for child protection within school will usually carry the main burden of this work.

During child protection work, schools may work directly or liaise with a range of agencies and professionals. Although the list that follows is not exhaustive, some examples of these agencies are:

- children's social care services – social workers, social work managers, foster carers, residential home carers
- police – specially training and non-uniformed officers from the local child protection police unit
- health – school nurse, health visitor, general practitioner (GP), therapists
- youth offending teams – officers supporting young people engaged with the criminal justice system
- housing – housing officers, where families live in local authority housing and where accommodation is relevant to the circumstances of the child

---

Prevention work with children in schools

In addition to their protective role, schools play a vital part in the prevention of abuse in the first place. Prevention work may include raising awareness among children of unacceptable behaviour they may encounter, and of how they can keep themselves safe. The guidance points out that Personal Social and Health Education (PSHE) provides opportunities to learn about such matters, as well as other practical issues such as who to ask for help if children feel unsafe. In addition, the guidance states that children should be taught how to recognize and manage risks and respond responsibly, how to distinguish acceptable from unacceptable physical contact, how to recognize unreasonable pressure from others and develop strategies for dealing with this, and how to use assertiveness techniques to resist pressure.

Generally speaking, the aim of such work is to give a clear message that any kind of violence or violation is unacceptable, and to let children know that asking for help is encouraged, and to point children to sources of help where appropriate. It is also important to listen to children, to provide appropriate spaces within school for this, to display national children's helpline numbers (e.g. Childline, NSPCC), and to use peer support schemes.

The role of schools in supporting children who have been abused

This is a further important area for schools, as most children subject to child protection measures remain living at home (Gibbons et al., 1995) and therefore, stay at the same school. With this in mind, the role of schools and settings in supporting children who have experienced abuse could include using existing relationships between children and staff so that the child knows someone cares about them. Staff can help the child, if necessary, to put responsibility for the abuse firmly with the abuser, and help answer any questions the child may have about what has happened. They can also support the child in developing protective strategies for the future, including assertiveness skills. Where children display disruptive behaviour, staff can support them to manage this. The curriculum can also be used to address such issues as individual rights and responsibilities or the importance of listening to others. In this way, individual children who have been abused may well feel supported in a way that avoids singling them out as different.

Responsibilities of individuals within schools

Guidance for any individual working with children, including school staff, can be found in the publication entitled 'What to do if you're worried a child is being abused' (DfES, 2006c). Every staff member should see it as their personal responsibility to promote the welfare of children in their school. Therefore, they should ensure they know who the designated officer for child protection is, and should familiarize themselves with the school's child protection policy. Within this, they should find out the system for recording and monitoring concerns. Furthermore, staff should attend any relevant child protection training on offer. Perhaps most important of all, staff should listen to children who may be trying to impart worrying information. They should then pass on the same to the designated officer. Individual staff need to realize that it is not their role to investigate any concerns, but to pass them on within school.

There are essentially three major elements to the individual being able to fulfil these responsibilities effectively: being alert to signs or indicators that may indicate harm, good monitoring and recording of events, and dealing appropriately with direct disclosures of harm from children. Each will be discussed in turn.

Signs and indicators of possible harm

It is neither possible nor desirable to attempt to produce a comprehensive checklist of every possible indicator of possible abuse. It is much more helpful for staff to think holistically. Signs of harm are only indicators of possible abuse and not proof of abuse – the bigger picture of the child is always more important. Where staff have a concern, they ask themselves what they already know about the child, any siblings, or the family which may help to explain the concerns. Some signs of abuse are common to all types of abuse; some are more specific to particular types of abuse. Furthermore, many indicators of possible harm are displayed by children at some time during the course of their lives. They may be reactions to distressing yet non-abusive experiences, for example witnessing an argument between their parents, moving house, the death of a pet and so on. It is important for staff to have abuse in their minds as a possibility without jumping to conclusions that the concerns observed must be the result of abuse.

It is important for staff to realize there is no stereotype of an abused child. Responses will vary between children and between the same children on different days. Some children, if subject to abuse, may become aggressive, disturbed or angry, others may become quiet or withdrawn. The same child may display aggression or withdrawal on different days, depending on their mood or their immediate experiences. Sudden changes in behaviour are particularly significant, and need some thought as to their origin. If a child who is usually ebullient and extrovert suddenly becomes quiet and withdrawn, or if a child, clean and dry during the day, suddenly begins wetting and soiling, questions would need to be asked as to possible reasons for this.

Relying on observations of children alone is one-dimensional. Staff should feel able to speak to colleagues (while maintaining sensitivity and confidentiality) or to the child. The important factor with the latter is how the child is spoken to – open questions that use the relationship with the child and which invite a full response should be asked, rather than closed questions which are likely only to elicit an unhelpful 'Yes' or 'No' response.

Monitoring and recording concerns

Schools have a responsibility to monitor the welfare of pupils and record any concerns which they may have about particular children. Generally these concerns should be shared and discussed with parents; however school staff can make a decision not to share such information if they believe that such sharing may place the child at increased risk of harm. This is more likely to be the case where the concerns relate to sexual or physical abuse, as the parents, if alerted, may react in a number of ways that could further harm the child, including removing them from school immediately (and hence place the child in the very situation that is deemed to be risky) or destroying evidence. The written child protection records should be held separately from educational records.

Monitoring concerns should help to clarify the nature and extent of the concerns by providing information on exactly what the concerns are and how long they have been of concern. Monitoring should provide a clear record of the development of concerns, by allowing a review of the child's progress over a number of weeks or even months. Patterns of behaviour can be identified, such as particular days on which behaviours or injuries are noticed. Clear records of concerns can contribute to the school making, where necessary, full, clear and professional referrals to children's social care services. Where all staff use the same system, consistency of recording is ensured.

Schools should monitor and record anything that they find worrying or inappropriate in relation to injuries, body language and behaviour, language and play, drawings and writing. Staff have to make a judgement about what is worrying or inappropriate, based on their experience, and knowledge of the child and family. Furthermore, any possible indications of neglect should be noted. Of course any direct disclosures of abuse from children need to be recorded.

Staff may make a record of the nature and quality of contact with parents. This could be particularly important if staff at the school have approached the parents about their concerns.

The response of the parents to these concerns could be an important part of the context when deciding the next step, or if making a referral to children's social care services.

Any records that are made should be factual, describing what was seen or said or heard. Opinions should be avoided where possible, but if they are recorded must be clearly flagged as such. Each record should give the day, date, time, and place of the incident. This helps to identify patterns of behaviour. The place could be crucial – if a child who is asked to collect paint from a store cupboard becomes distressed while in there, this should be recorded, as it may be that their entering the cupboard has triggered an emotional reaction to a previous experience of, say, being locked in a cupboard. It may be helpful at times for the record to contain brief relevant background information to contextualize the concern. Any words the child says should be recorded word for word. Although there may be a temptation to do so, staff should never change any words used, particularly for parts of the body. The main reason for this is to maintain clarity and accuracy of recording. Staff should keep any initial notes, however untidily written. Sometimes, a member of staff will hear or notice something about a child while preoccupied, and may scribble initial notes on any piece of paper which is to hand. This should then be transferred to a formal monitoring sheet as soon as possible; however the initial scribbled notes should also be kept to demonstrate that the recording was made contemporaneously (at the time of the incident) and not some hours or days later. This could be particularly important if the case ends up in court, and a solicitor questions the validity of the incident.

Activity 8.2

At the end of school one day, a mother of a five-year-old girl arrives to collect her. The class teacher is concerned the mother is under the influence of alcohol and decides to make a note of this. She completes a standard monitoring form with the day, date and time, and writes 'When Mum came to collect her daughter, she was drunk'.

Discussion
There is good practice here in that the teacher uses the correct form and records when the concern arose. However, her statement is an opinion. What is 'drunk'? It does not explain why the staff member was concerned. The teacher could have written 'When Mum came to collect her daughter, her breath smelled of alcohol, her speech was incoherent, and she was staggering about. In my opinion, she was drunk'. This is factual, describing what was seen, and why the staff member was concerned about it. It is a much more powerful piece of evidence than the first statement.

Dealing with a disclosure from a child

Quite different from staff noticing concerns about children that may or may not be tantamount to abuse, is the matter of a child making a clear disclosure of abuse. It is important that school staff are clear about how best to respond to such occasions.

Before or when a child speaks, the staff member should never enter into a pact of secrecy with them. The staff member should explain they may have to pass information on to help keep the child safe. If the child then declines to speak further, the adult should not pursue this, but should let the child know they are there for them whenever they need support. As the child speaks, the adult should stay calm and not show strong emotions. The chief reason for this is that, if such emotions are expressed, the child may well think that it is they, and not the incident, that has made the adult shocked or angry and so on. The staff member may need to express such feelings appropriately to colleagues or a supervisor after the event and receive appropriate support for this; however to do so in front of the child would be wholly inappropriate.

The adult should reassure the child throughout the exchange. This may include telling them they are pleased; they are telling them about what has happened, that they are doing well, and that they can see how difficult it is. The adult should encourage the child to talk but avoid asking leading questions. The use of such encouraging phrases as 'Go on' or simply 'Yes' can be effective here, as can the consistent use of open questions. Open or indirect questions invite the child to give a statement. These are to be contrasted with closed or direct questions which usually only elicit a 'Yes' or 'No' answer, and which are unhelpful. Open questions could include 'What happened next?', 'Can you say more about that?', 'How did that come about?' and so on. Similar questions, when asked in a closed manner, and therefore to be avoided, could include 'Did they hit you?', 'Have you finished?', 'Was it your father who did that to you?' This last question is particularly poor as it is suggesting an individual who may be responsible, and if the child answers in the affirmative, it is unclear if they fully understand the question and its implications, and whether the child is merely answering in a way they think the adult would like to hear. In and among these open questions, it is also acceptable, even advisable, for the adult to check that they have understood correctly what the child is trying to say. This could involve the adult summarizing the child's words. Where children, for whatever reason (and this may be particularly relevant to staff in special schools or early years settings) do not possess the complexity of language, it is acceptable to use more direct questions in relation to the context of the abuse, but not to the abuse itself. Examples of such appropriate direct questions might be to clarify the time of day, such as 'Was it before lunch or after lunch?' or 'Was it light or dark?' These kinds of questions can be very helpful in assisting the child to locate in their memory and experience the actual abuse while also helping the adult to fully contextualize the situation.

The adult should not tell the child that what has happened to them is naughty or bad, as the child may well hear these words and assume that they have been naughty or bad. The adult can use phrases as 'What happened to you was wrong'. This could be particularly helpful to the child if they feel partly responsible for or guilty about the abuse occurring. The child needs to know abuse is never their fault, even if they partly feel it is or might be. Furthermore, the adult should not make any comment about the alleged offender beyond, perhaps, that they were wrong to do as they did. To begin to berate the perpetrator using expletives or derogatory language is not only unprofessional, it is also inappropriate since the offender may well be someone, like a parent, whom the child loves. Once again, the adult may need to sound off appropriately with colleagues and receive support about this.

Even if the child, having made a clear disclosure, then retracts what they have said, it is essential for the adult to report all that they have heard. A child may, on making the disclosure, feel they are betraying the abuser, or they may have been told that if they tell someone, terrible things will happen to all concerned. This may cause the child to panic once the disclosure is made, and to retract it. Having let the cat out of the bag, they may try to put it back in. However, a child cannot 'unmake' a disclosure, and it should be passed on for others to make a decision as to its validity.

As soon as possible after the disclosure, the adult concerned should make a detailed record of the conversation, following the guidelines for recording discussed above. The disclosure must be passed on immediately to the designated staff member who should pass it on to children's social care services as soon as possible.

Activity 8.3

Sarah is nine years old, white British and attends her local primary school where she is in Year 4. School has had no concerns about her whatsoever. One day, she asks her teacher that if she tells her something, can the teacher promise to keep it a secret? The teacher explains she cannot promise this, and says that depending on what it is, she may have to pass it on so the school can help. Sarah goes on to disclose sexual abuse by her stepfather. The teacher stays calm and does not show any emotions. She allows Sarah to tell her story, occasionally reassuring her and encouraging her through the use of phrases such as 'Go on' and 'I can see this is difficult, you are doing really well.' At one point the teacher asks Sarah 'Did your stepfather touch your bottom?' to which she replies 'Yes'. Sarah goes on to say that he also touched her 'front bottom'. The teacher, who has already agreed with Sarah at the beginning of the interview that she will make some notes, records *Stepfather touched her vagina.* At the end, Sarah suddenly says that actually she was being silly and has just made it all up to get her stepfather into trouble because he was cross with her last night. The teacher thanks Sarah and explains that she will still have to pass on the information. She writes up the discussion fully and gives this to the designated officer, who makes a referral to social services.

Can you identify good practice in how the teacher dealt with this disclosure?

Can you see any areas which could have been handled better?

Safeguarding adults who attend schools and colleges

Legally, an adult is anyone over the age of 17. Adults of 18 years and above may well attend mainstream schools (during the second year of 'A'-levels), special schools (usually up to the age of 19) or mainstream and specialist further education colleges (again, usually no further than up to the age of 19).

Safeguarding children procedures do not apply to adults, even where those adults remain in full-time education. Nevertheless, of course, some of these adults may need protecting from harm. There are at least two key national documents relevant to the protection of adults. The first is a government document entitled 'No secrets' (DH, 2000); the second, produced by a national social care organization, builds on this and is called 'Safeguarding adults' (Association of Directors of Social Services, 2005). Neither of these are designed to deal in detail with adults in education, and in fact are weighted either in favour of adults in the community in receipt of social care services or in residential or nursing homes. Nevertheless, the key principles are applicable to adults in education. Many of the procedures outlined within them follow a very similar pattern to safeguarding children procedures discussed above and so do not require repeating. Generally speaking, staff in schools and colleges should follow a very similar process for responding for concerns about adult students as they do for children. One interesting and useful extension of safeguarding children documentation is that within the notion of safeguarding adults, other forms of abuse apart from physical, sexual, emotional and neglect should be considered. These are financial or material abuse, and discriminatory abuse (based on racism, sexism etc.).

One of the key issues here is the possible tension between the choice and independence of the adult concerned, and the responsibility of the staff member to respond to any concerns. With children, the adult can justifiably override the child's wishes where necessary and report their concerns on the grounds that it is in the child's interests to do so. This is based on the notion that the child may not fully comprehend the consequences of inaction. However, with adults in education, this argument becomes more complex. Generally speaking, adults are deemed to fully understand the consequences of their actions and a distinction is thus drawn between those adults who, according to the Mental Capacity Act 2005, have 'mental capacity' and those who do not. Adults are deemed to have mental capacity if they can make decisions for themselves. A lack of mental capacity can be permanent or temporary.

Where adults have mental capacity, and can take full responsibility for their own actions and its consequences, the role of the staff member in education becomes one of supporter, of provider of information to help them live as safely as possible and so on.

Where adults do not have mental capacity, schools and colleges are authorized to make decisions on their behalf, just as they would for children. Among all of this, of course, is the inherent difficulty of deciding which adults have mental capacity or not – for some it will be obvious but there will be any number of adults whose mental capacity may be difficult to establish, despite the full guidelines offered in Section Three of the Mental Capacity Act 2005.

Activity 8.4

Peter is aged 18 and has mild learning disabilities. He lives at home with both parents and attends college. A staff member notices that he arrives at college with bruising to his arms. Peter explains that sometimes his father gets frustrated with him and shouts at him and grips and punches his arms. Peter is adamant that he does not want the staff member to do anything about this. He says he likes living at home and is worried about being made to live in a shared group home. He says he generally gets on with his parents and these incidents are isolated.

Do you think Peter has mental capacity?

How do you think the staff member should respond to this situation?

Summary

- Child protection is now seen as a sub-set of a broader approach to safeguard and promote the welfare of children.
- Some children attending school are likely to experience harm or abuse in their home lives. This possibility needs to inform the response of schools when concerns about children are noted.
- Schools should have a written child protection policy and a designated person for child protection who takes the lead in ensuring the school has correct systems and procedures in place, and that all individuals within school take appropriate responsibility.
- Where vulnerable adults in education may require protecting, staff need to try to determine whether these adults have 'mental capacity' meaning they can make decisions for themselves. Only where staff deem vulnerable adults not to have such mental capacity, can staff make decisions on behalf of the adult concerned.

References

Association of Directors of Social Services (2005) *Safeguarding Adults: A National Framework of Standards for Good Practice and Outcomes in Adult Protection Work.* London: The Association of Directors of Social Services

Baginsky, M (2000) *Child Protection and Education.* London: NSPCC

Corwin Sanders, C and Hendry, L B (1997) *New Perspectives on Disaffection.* London: Cassel

Cawson, P, Wattam, C, Brooker, S and Kelly, G (2000) *Child Maltreatment in the UK: A Study of the Prevalence of Child Abuse and Neglect.* London: NSPCC

DfES (Department for Education and Skills) (2003) *Every Child Matters.* London: The Stationery Office

DfES (Department for Education and Skills) (2006a) *Working Together to Safeguard Children: A Guide to Inter-agency Working to Safeguard and Promote the Welfare of Children.* Norwich: The Stationery Office

DfES (Department for Education and Skills) (2006b) *Safeguarding Children and Safer Recruitment in Education.* Nottingham: DfES Publications

DfES (Department for Education and Skills) (2006c) *What to do if you're Worried a Child is Being Abused.* Nottingham: DfES Publications

DH (Department of Health) (2000) *No Secrets: Guidance on Developing and Implementing Multi-Agency Policies and Procedures to Protect Vulnerable Adults from Abuse.* London: Department of Health

DH (Department of Health) (2002) *Women's Mental Health: Into the Mainstream – Strategic Development of Mental Health Care for Women.* London: Department of Health

DH, DfEE and HO (Department of Health, Department for Education and Employment and Home Office) (2000) *Framework for the Assessment of Children in Need and their Families.* London: The Stationery Office

Furlong, A and Cartmel, F (2007) *Young People and Social Change: New Perspectives.* London. Open University Press

Gibbons, J, Conroy, S and Bell, C (1995) *Operating the Child Protection System: A Study of Child Protection Practices in English Local Authorities.* London: HMSO

Hanvey, C (2003) 'The lessons we never learn', [Internet]. http://www.guardian.co.uk/society/2003/jan/26/comment. childprotection: (accessed 22 June 2007)

National Commission of Inquiry into the Prevention of Child Abuse (1996) *Childhood Matters: Report of the National Commission of Inquiry into the Prevention of Child Abuse*, Volume 1: the Report. London: The Stationery Office

Further reading

Beckett, C (2003) *Child Protection: An Introduction.* London: Sage

Flynn, H and Starns, B (2004) *Protecting Children: Working Together to Keep Children Safe.* London: Heinemann

Whitney, B (2004) *Protecting Children: A Handbook for Teachers and School Managers.* London: RoutledgeFalmer

Useful websites

www.dfes.gov.uk/rsgateway/ – Department for children, schools and families: research and statistics publications gateway. The site contains a host of factual information on a range of topics. There is a useful search engine allowing easy access to information.

www.everychildmatters.gov.uk/socialcare/safeguarding/ – Every Child Matters: safeguarding children. This section of the huge Every Child Matters site provides guidance on a range of matters concerned with child protection.

www.teachernet.gov.uk/wholeschool/familyandcommunity/childprotection – Teachernet: child protection. This site is dedicated to the role of schools in child protection and contains much useful information, advice and guidance.

www.nspcc.org.uk/Inform/trainingandconsultancy/Training/TrainingCourses/trainingcourses_wda47913.html – The National Society for the Prevention of Cruelty to Children (NSPCC) training website, which outlines the range of training courses they provide.

Useful internet search terms

child protection
safeguarding children
child protection policy
national guidance on safeguarding
safeguarding adults
mental capacity

9 Disaffection, Society and Education

Barbara Murphy

Introduction

In August 2007, around 30,000 pupils left school with no GCSEs at all to their name; undoubtedly undesirable in an age when formal qualifications of increasing complexity are required for practically any employment prospects. Alarmingly, this appears not to be an isolated event, with statistics (DfES, 2007) indicating that during each year of the past decade around 1 in 5 young people have left compulsory schooling without qualifications, training or a job. Studies (Raffe, 2003: 6) indicate, perhaps unsurprisingly, that such young people are highly likely to exhibit poor attitudes to school and schooling and that many have truanted or have been excluded at some point during their school careers. Dramatic press headlines meanwhile, highlight the apparent rising involvement of young people in crime epidemics and criminal activity which has led to a widespread castigation of young people in the public press and a concern that the 'social fabric' (Furlong, 2007: 104) of society is breaking down. From such evidence it might be concluded that a significant body of young people are disaffected not just from education, but from the norms and values of society as a whole. As Bunting (2007) comments:

> Elections were once won or lost on economic issues, now it's social issues; the detail of parenting policies and youth work have migrated from the derided margins of political debate to the centre. David Cameron adapts Bill Clinton's catchphrase, 'It's the society, stupid'.

This chapter will examine the complex interplay between individual, institutional and socio-cultural factors contributing towards educational disaffection within our society.

A changing society?

Most (Furlong, 2007; Giddens, 1991; Sanders and Hendry, 1997) agree that the experiences of young people have changed radically over recent decades, with one of the key characteristics being that in today's society transition phases – such as the transition from babyhood to childhood, from childhood to teenager and from teenager to adult – tend to be far less predicable and more fragmented than in previous decades. The smooth negotiation of these stages is widely agreed to be important not only to the effective social development of the individual concerned but also to wider social inclusion and, crucially, to the construction of an adult identity within society (Corwin Sanders, 1997: 10). Coles (1995) and Furlong (2007: 53) identify that most modern societies confer adult status to young people only after the completion of a relatively lengthy phase which involves a number of transitions, including the transition from school to work and then to independent living. This phase, which during the 1960s and 1970s was influenced by a judicious mix of the conventions of society (marriage, a steady job) and by social class, led to relatively predictable and stable outcomes and young people in most developed nations were generally able to gain a significant degree of financial and personal independence by their late teens (Coles, 1995; Kiernan, 1992). However, the gradual erosion of such conventions within society, combined with the economics of a post-industrial nation which restricts the employment opportunities of unqualified young people primarily to poorly paid and insecure jobs within the service industry together with increased housing costs has meant that many young people today are essentially forced into a state of semi-dependency, moving backwards and forwards into a variety of living arrangements. In this way the transition to adult status is blurred and may not be completed until much later in life than in previous decades, resulting in a somewhat uneasy balance between dependency and autonomy (Furlong, 2007: 56). Adding to this general confusion is the sheer number of contradictions within our society regarding the age at which adult status might be considered to be reached.

Activity 9.1 Becoming an Adult

When exactly does a young person become an adult in our society? At 16? 17? 18? Later? Find out and note down what 16, 17 and 18 year olds can and cannot do at the current time. Consider such things as the age at which a young person can drive, drink, smoke, vote as well as the age of consent, and the age at which you can make a will or buy a house. Wikipedia: 'Youth Rights' may be useful as a source of information.

Identify the variety of messages that are given regarding the transition to adult status in our society. How might these contradictions create difficulties for young people during this phase of their lives?

The transition period from teenager to adult is often regarded as a time of relative freedom from adult responsibilities and an opportunity to make the most of life. Societal changes in recent decades have resulted in the widely held expectation that individuals are responsible for the creation of their own lifestyle; pieced together from the bewildering range of options and choices available. This rise in the individualization of lifestyle is considered to create an element of *risk* to the individual concerned, not least of all because of the uncertainty integral to each element of choice. For this reason it can be surmised (Furlong, 2007: 144) that we live in an increasingly risky society. There is wide agreement, however, that there is considerable inequality in the distribution of choices and thus the likelihood of risk throughout our society. Broadly speaking, poverty tends to involve less opportunity for choice and tends to attract risks, whereas wealth buys relative freedom from risk and offers more potential for choice (Beck, 1992: 35). Individuals from less economically advantaged backgrounds are more likely to have access to a restricted range of choices which may then limit the productive use of this transition period, increasing the risk of disaffection. For some, street socializing becomes the only choice available. Although 'hanging out' with mates is something that most groups of all social classes will do, and indeed social groupings are an important and normal component of society as a whole and a means by which an individual helps create their personal and collective identity, street socialization is usually a temporary phase confined to middle adolescence. There is some indication (Macdonald and Marsh, 2006) that street socialization as a sole and maintained form of leisure choice places severe constraints on the opportunities for individuals within these groups to form wider and more socially varied friendships; which may result in the construction of substitute tribal, or gang, identity. Gang identity not only tends to delay the formation of adult identity but is also strongly predicative of involvement with anti-social or criminal activities, meaning that such individuals are significantly at risk of becoming disaffected from the norms of society. In all, social class continues to exert a powerful influence in society and there continues to be a strong link between social class, disadvantage and disaffection. An uneasy relationship between choices, risk, poverty and disaffection is created when everything, in terms of life choices, is presented as a possibility but where in reality the choices, particularly for those individuals from lower socio-economic groups (Rutter and Smith, 1995), are severely constrained.

Sweeping generalizations, however, cannot be made about youth, nor social class. *All* young people have to negotiate the risky business of growing up and the vast majority from all social classes do so successfully. Nevertheless there is considerable consensus (Klein, 2000; McDowell, 2003; Roberts, 1995) regarding the way in which transient 'McJobs' have significantly reduced job security for the very least qualified young people and the impact that this has had on the transition from school to work. In this way, young people who are disaffected with school, who leave with little to show for their years of compulsory education and thus who have poor job prospects are not only disadvantaged, but are at risk of becoming more widely disaffected both with and from society. The links between disaffection with education, educational achievement, and wider disaffection from society are clear cut.

Without doubt the educational system plays a crucial role in enabling young people to gain appropriate qualifications that will enhance the possibility of secure employment, breaking the cycle of disadvantage and disaffection. As Riddell (2007) argues, 'society's monsters are often also frightened kids, allowed to fail and fall from infancy'.

Failing pupils – or a failing system?

The majority of primary school pupils appear to enjoy school. Problems with disengagement and disaffection are most evident during secondary schooling and the bulk of formal exclusions occur during these years (DfES, 2005), with a peak reached at the age of 15: year 10 of compulsory education. Studies, (Hendry et al., 1993; Keys et al., 1995; Riley and Docking 2004) indicate that, at this age, although the majority of pupils place a high value on education, just 11 per cent find the taught curriculum interesting. Girls, who generally seem more positive than boys about their experiences in school (Riley, 2002: 173), appear to be more tolerant of school systems and structures and disaffected pupils are predominately male. So what is it about the school system that is so intolerable? Various studies conducted with pupils at risk of disaffection found that a wide variety of factors, including poor relationships and interactions with teachers, crumbling and uninviting school environments, the poor attitudes and behaviour of their peers, an unappealing curriculum and tedious lessons all contribute towards turning pupils off school; but of these, that relationships with *teachers* appear to be crucial (Kinder et al., 1996; Riley and Docking, 2004: 172). In particular, teachers who 'talk down' to pupils, shout, place blame unfairly or who show little respect for individuals seem to play a significant role in triggering disaffection in vulnerable individuals. When combined with inflexible school rules and limited opportunities to express views and opinions these traits appear to be sufficient to 'tip the balance in [...] behaviour and send (pupils) spiralling down the path of exclusion'. (Riley, 2002: 12). Many pupils in Riley's study also considered that their specific learning needs were insufficiently addressed within the classroom, citing inadequate support and poor or absent differentiation all of which profoundly affected their ability to engage with the curriculum and to achieve success, leading to their eventual disengagement. For these pupils, inadequate and inappropriate school systems and structures seem to play a significant role in their failure to engage with the process of education.

Looking at Research 9.1: Student's Experiences of Ability Grouping

Dispiritingly, a number of recent studies, for example that conducted by Boaler (2000) have indicated that the widespread adoption of 'setting' by ability in both primary and secondary schools appears to contribute significantly and negatively towards pupil motivation, engagement and achievement in

Looking at Research 9.1—cont'd

lessons at all levels of attainment. This comprehensive report, which involved over 120 hours of mathematics lesson observations and interviews with 72 students, presents a worrying picture of a 'continuous diet of low level work' for students in lower sets:

> L: *We come in, sit down and there's work on the board and he just says copy it. I think it's all too easy.*
> R: *It's far too easy.*
> I (Interviewer): *What happens if it's too easy? Do they make it any harder?*
> M: *No, we just have to carry on. We just have to do it. If you refuse to do it he'll just give a detention. It's just so easy.* (Boaler, 2000: 638)

Students in upper sets, meanwhile, typically report being required to learn at a pace that, for many, seemed incompatible with understanding. These students were often very unhappy with the teaching in the top set, but recognized the status that this conferred on them. Observations showed that teachers of the top sets 'raced through the examples on the board, speaking quickly, often interjecting their speech with phrases such as "come on we haven't got much time" and "just do this quickly" ' (ibid.: 635).

The authors conclude that setting primarily did not seem to do the job that it was designed to do and that there were considerable disadvantages, not least of all that it could be the 'single most important cause of low levels of achievement' (ibid.: 646).

While many disaffected pupils clearly experience difficulties in accessing the taught curriculum, the unwieldy, restrictive and prescriptive nature of the taught curriculum appears to aggravate this further. In 2006, the Minister for school standards, David Miliband, cited boredom of the academic curriculum as 'the biggest cause of pupils losing interest in school' (BBC News, 2006) and indeed, a common theme expressed by pupils was the perception that the school curriculum appeared irrelevant to their experiences and needs. This, combined with a 'disadvantaging combination of coursework and examinations' (Solomon and Rogers, 2001: 333) undoubtedly contributes significantly towards pupil disaffection with school during the secondary years, but the profound influence of individual and personal factors such as general motivation, self-esteem and self-efficacy and their role within this equation need to be considered carefully.

A considerable body of research into disaffection has focused on individual and personal factors and their relationship to learning (Hidi and Harackiewicz, 2000; Solomon and Rogers, 2001) and a number of early studies indicated some correlation between self-esteem and academic achievement. As low academic achievement is strongly predictive of potential disaffection with school (Bailey, 2005: 1; Solomon, 2001: 331), it could be surmised that poor self-esteem is directly related to disaffection. More recent studies (Muijs, 1997; Ross, 2000), however, indicate that while academic achievement appears to improve self-esteem; high self-esteem, in isolation from other factors, is not strongly predictive of academic success.

Looking at Research 9.2: Being in Control

Ross's comprehensive study takes a critical stance in their examination of the increasingly commonly held truism that 'self esteem has replaced understanding as the goal of education'. (Kramer, 1991: 210)

The authors argue that this idea is misplaced and that there is little evidence to suggest that simply 'feeling good about oneself' will directly improve the academic achievement of young people. Rather, they suggest, learners who feel *in control* of important outcomes in their lives, who believe that their own efforts and actions shape their successes and failures are more likely to achieve success.

This premise was examined through a combination of student questionnaires and performance in national tests, with the conclusion that an individual's sense of being in control *did* appear to significantly affect subsequent test results, but that high self-esteem, although often derived from successful performance in national tests, was not at all predictive of subsequent academic success.

In conclusion, then, a focus on improving pupil's self-esteem, in isolation from other affecting factors, is highly unlikely to provide a magic bullet solution to disaffection.

The need for an individual to 'feel in control' is examined in recent studies of human motivational dynamics (Weiner, 1984 in Docking, 1990) and this has pertinent relevance to the ways in which pupils at risk of disaffection become increasingly disengaged and alienated from school practice. In particular, studies examining theories of *attribution* are useful in understanding this process. Such studies indicate that if an individual tends to attribute the failure of a task to a stable cause such as lack of ability, or success in a task to an external and unstable cause such as help from a teacher, then this is likely to produce expectations for more of the same as both are outside the boundaries of personal control. The sustained attribution of the reason for success or failure to factors that the individual is powerless to change is then highly likely to result in a cycle of 'learned helplessness' with continued low expectations, educational underachievement and potential disaffection. Effort, however, is widely considered to be a controllable factor and thus the lack of effort typically displayed by disaffected pupils may be explained in terms of human motivational dynamics as an attempt to be in control of the situation: if I don't try, I don't fail.

The role of control is also evident in studies exploring the effect of the school environment and ethos on pupil motivation. Such studies demonstrate beyond doubt that the school environment and ethos have a powerful effect on pupil attitude and engagement. The types of ethos most likely to disengage students include 'controlling' environments in which the outcomes and goals appear to be set by other people and 'amotivating' environments whereby the individual is led to believe that they have not got the capabilities to succeed (Deci and Ryan, 1985 in Docking, 1990: 89). Both of these types of environments are amply evident within the current educational system; a system in which the outcomes and goals of compulsory education appear to be largely decided by political agendas and one in which the focus on high academic standards effectively alienates and fails vulnerable young people.

Troubled . . . intolerable, or just not tolerated?

Exclusion from school, which generally follows a long 'tail' of persistently poor behaviour (Gordon, 2001: 76; Parsons, 1999) is generally regarded as being the most public manifestation of disaffection from schooling.

Table 9.1 shows the number of permanent exclusions in England from 1990.

Abundantly evident in these figures is the fourfold rise in exclusions between 1990 and 1998. However, for every pupil who is excluded permanently it is estimated there are around ten fixed-term exclusions; meaning that the pupil concerned is excluded from school for a fixed number of days. If these figures were included it is estimated (Gordon, 2001; Parsons, 1999; Smith, 1998) that the total number of pupils formally excluded from the education system would approach 1 per cent of all school pupils. Additionally, if informal exclusions, such as those pupils who are voluntarily withdrawn from school (Gordon, 2001: 71) or who self exclude through truancy (Reid estimates that between 600,000 and 1.2 million pupils truant daily) or those who are informally excluded in a multitude of other ways are

Table 9.1 Permanent exclusion in England

	Permanent Exclusions		
	Boys	**Girls**	**Total**
Number of exclusions			
Age (4):			
4 and under	20	#	20
5	50	10	50
6	80	10	90
7	150	10	160
8	210	10	230
9	350	20	370
10	390	20	410
11	590	90	680
12	1,240	300	1,540
13	1,900	570	2,470
14	2,080	670	2,750
15	860	210	1,070
16	20	#	30
17	10	10	20

Source: DfES National Statistics SFR 23/2005

included, it is clear that this is a significant problem both nationally and socially. (Reid, 2005 in Topping and Maloney, 2005: 115)

Parsons (1999: 187) questions whether these pupils are 'troubled . . . intolerable, or just not tolerated?' and explains the rise in exclusions as a direct consequence of the increased individualization of society. Here poor behaviour is seen as an individual's *choice* and thus this inappropriate choice must be punished. Docking (1990: 140) also discuss the rise in formal exclusions in terms of the relatively recent 'zero tolerance' stance adopted by society and discuss the pressure on schools, as microcosms of society, to adopt a similar stance. Others point to the increased pressure placed on schools during the 1990s; a decade which saw huge changes in school accountability in terms of examination results, OFSTED inspections and league tables, to achieve high academic results, arguably at the expense of a less measurable caring and inclusive philosophy. Exclude the troublesome pupils and the examination results improve! The noticeable fall in exclusion figures during 1999 is widely thought to be a consequence of the publication in that year of statutory guidance setting punitive exclusion targets for schools (DfEE, 1999) and there is some evidence (Gordon, 2001: 70) that this resulted in a number of schools under-reporting formal exclusion rates largely through the adoption of informal, often voluntary, exclusion strategies.

So, who are the excluded pupils? Although all social classes are represented, boys from lower socio-economic groups predominate and approximately four boys are excluded for every girl. Studies, such as that carried out by the New Policy Institute in 2006, indicates that from an early age boys tend to exhibit more directionally challenging behaviour, react to conflict more aggressively than girls (who often have better communication skills and seem able to talk their way out of difficulty) and that this results in more severe disciplinary sanctions. However, although girls represent just 17 per cent of all formal exclusions, there is growing concern that there are far higher numbers of girls who are unofficially excluded, particularly through truancy (ibid.). Traveller and looked after children are significantly over-represented in exclusion figures, and there has long been concern over the consistent proportional over-representation of Black boys in these. Black pupils, who represent just 2 per cent of the school population, are around five times more likely to be excluded than Caucasian pupils (Gordon, 2001: 74; Parsons, 1999: 136) and there is some suggestion (Sewell, 1997 in Parsons, 1999: 136) that this may be in part due to teacher's responses to cultural differences in behaviour and attitude.

Activity 9.2 Girls and Exclusion

Nationally, girls comprise just 17 per cent of permanent exclusions, although we know that many more are unofficially and informally excluded. As a result their needs have tended to be overlooked in school exclusion strategies. What effect might this have on girls' experiences in the classroom? How might this impact on their attitudes to school?

Table 9.2 shows the ages of pupils permanently excluded during 2004–2005.

Disturbingly, in this period 20 children under the age of 4 were permanently excluded from their schools with undoubtedly huge consequences to both the individuals and the families concerned. Nevertheless the numbers of primary aged children excluded from school are relatively small and the figures appear to be remarkably stable over time (Pavey and Visser, 2003: 182). Problems with disaffection are most apparent towards the end of compulsory schooling, although without doubt the far higher exclusion rates seen at this stage are 'manifestations of a process initiated much earlier' (Bailey, 2005: 1), involving a wide range of individual, social and cultural factors. There is some consensus however, that the differences in exclusion rates may be partially due to the inherent differences between primary and secondary schools. Not only do the majority of primary head teachers tend to view exclusion as essentially ineffective for the pupils concerned (Pavey and Visser, 2003: 185), but the majority of primary schools are relatively small and class teachers tend to have sustained contact with one class. This model is much more likely to enable the development of supportive and individual relationships with pupils, which most agree is crucial in the prevention of disaffection. As Munn and Lloyd (2005: 208) argues, disaffected young people 'want to be seen as people. They want teachers to understand their home circumstances and they want respect'. The model of a single class teacher with visiting subject teachers has recently been adopted for early secondary pupils by a small, but growing number of UK secondary schools with encouraging results in terms of the development of close relationships between pupils and the class teacher and improved pupil attitudes to work (Thomas, 2007).

Exclusion is an important issue for a number of reasons. Not only is the financial cost to schools, the health services, social services and the criminal justice system, at estimated

Table 9.2 Permanent exclusion in England

Year	Exclusions
1990–91	2,910
1991–92	3,833
1992–93	8,636
1993–94	11,181
1994–95	12,458
1995–98	Circa 12,500 p/a
1998–99	10,440
1999–00	8,300
2000–01	9,410
2001–02	9,540
2002–03	9,290
2003–04	9,880
2004–05	9,440

Source: DfES, National Statistics online, 2005

£81 million per annum (Parsons, 1999), excessive, but the cost to the individual may be immense. Pupils excluded from school for long periods of time may be effectively 'deschooled' making reintegration virtually impossible. Only around 27 per cent of excluded pupils of secondary age return to mainstream education, while a further 30 per cent attend Pupil Referral Units (PRUs), which often provide just half-time education. The remaining 30 per cent are educated at home, typically for a mere 5–10 hours per week. Arguably (Parsons, 1999: 138 in Topping and Maloney, 2005) excluded pupils need *more*, not less, time with professionals in order to fully address their needs, which include a multitude of educational, social and emotional problems. Failure to provide this time may be considered to be yet another way in which the English social, cultural and educational system effectively alienates vulnerable young people still further.

Curriculum initiatives

Undoubtedly the current educational system and in particular the drive to raise standards has played a central part in the development of pupil disengagement (Cullingford and Oliver, 2001: 132; Riley, 2004: 177) and for these reasons it makes sense to advocate caution in the adoption of purely curriculum focused strategies for reducing disaffection. Indeed whether or not it is actually possible to design a curriculum that fulfils the needs of all stakeholders in education is in itself contestable (Cullingford, 2001: 87). Nevertheless there is considerable consensus (Reid, 2002: 153) that a more flexible and relevant curriculum, in particular a more work-based or vocational curriculum, may begin to address aspects of pupil disaffection with school.

In 2004, the DfES white paper set out a basic entitlement for the 'disapplication' of two GCSE subjects to be replaced by a placement providing work-based learning. As Charles Clark, the then minister for Education argued:

> Relaxing the sometimes over-rigid demands of the National Curriculum after 14 so that children can follow courses which they enjoy, and on which they thrive (may be better) than forcing them to study subjects in which they have no interest or aptitude.

Recent studies however, have demonstrated that work-based placements are widely viewed as being suitable mostly for pupils at significant risk of exclusion, are disproportionately experienced by working class pupils and pupils with Special Educational Needs and also carry the associated risk that pupils who experience these may be even further 'marginalised' from the main education system (Green, 1991). Nevertheless, the benefits of work-related learning are widely considered (Ofsted, 1998) to include improved attitudes to school, together with a better understanding of the need to develop the 'soft' skills valued by employers, such as team work and the ability to relate to others. A number of caveats exist, however, and these include the premise that placements should not only offer real opportunities to engage with the work offered, develop specific skills and offer a quality work-based experience, but also that they should lead somewhere: directly to college courses, apprenticeships, or a job. In recent years apprenticeships and practical employment-based learning have increasingly been marginalized from main stream education and are seen very much as the option for those who are not *capable* of an academic education, whereas a number of other European countries, in particular Germany, run an alliance of vocational and mainstream education which is widely regarded as both sensible and successful. Initial proposals for a similar system in the United Kingdom proposed by Tomlinson in 2004 (DfES, 2004b) included a radical reworking of the English qualifications systems for 14–19 year olds that removed both GCSEs and A-levels entirely; thus completely replacing a structure regarded in some quarters as a 'system of selection at 16' (Hodgson and Spours, 2005: 9). This, however, proved to be rather too contentious for the UK government of the time (ibid.) and from 2005 to the present day the proposals have been revised extensively to produce a unified but arguably hybrid, system of vocational diplomas, traditional GCSEs and other established qualifications with an attempt to establish parity and standardization between the various routes (DfES, 2007).

Figure 9.1 illustrates the proposed structure of the qualifications pathway (DfES, 2007).

The underlying principles of such a wide-ranging reform are undoubtedly secure and rightly include the vision that all young people should be entitled to access all and any route at a level that is right for them. Such reform certainly has a number of potential benefits, including improved chances of employment and less risk of social exclusion at a young age (DfES, 2007: 5), but is not entirely without critics. In particular, the expectation that schools and colleges of further education work in partnership with employers has led to a

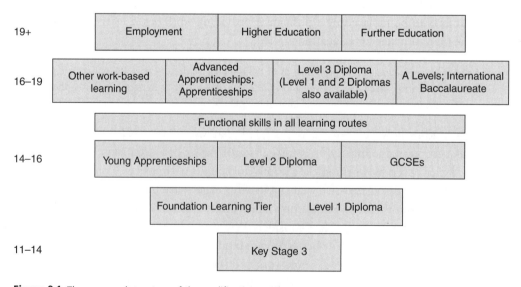

Figure 9.1 The proposed structure of the qualifications pathway.
Source: DfES, 2007

number of concerns that the vocational diplomas, which are central to the reform and cover broad themes such as engineering, creative and media, health and social care and construction will essentially be 'on the job training' as opposed to education. There is considerable debate over the decision to retain GCSEs and A-levels, which some, including Hodgson and Spours (2005), argue 'freezes' the system in its traditional 'culture of selection, division and failure' (Hodgson and Spours, 2005: 2) and that essentially the reform boils down to the creation of a vocational route for less academic learners who are not 'willing or able' to do GCSEs and A-levels. Thus, rather than being true curriculum reform, this could be argued to be a short-term solution unlikely to address the 'legacy of failure' (ibid.) of secondary schooling in England and additionally one that raises questions as to whether this is essentially yet another form of selection. If GCSEs and A-levels continue to be viewed in England as having more 'status' than vocational qualifications and thus more suitable for progression to higher education, key issues arise around the potentially divisive process of identifying pupils as 'less academic' and therefore more suitable for a vocational route and to the genuine feasibility of a return to an academic route at a later stage, should the need arise (ibid.). Despite assurances of parity of experience (DfES, 2007), it seems unlikely that this can be ensured given the considerable difficulty of devising comparable programmes of study that cover a diverse and disparate range of vocational areas and that address the various requirements of employers. It could be surmised that pupils who take the vocational route will be essentially, from the age of 14, denied access to the traditional 'broad and balanced curriculum' that includes a knowledge and understanding of languages, culture and the arts, and that is widely considered to form an essential basis of knowledge and understanding that enables individuals to take their place in our society. Young (1993: 203) however, argues that today's curriculum, which has barely changed in content and form since the beginnings of compulsory education, is outdated and is no longer fit for purpose in the twenty-first century, a view that has considerable support in some quarters. Hayton (2004: 221) surmises that a 'curriculum with its links to the world outside school would make schools less likely to produce an excluded group, disaffected from the curriculum and any kind of learning' but, crucially, concludes that this would have to be a two-way process that involved changes to societies' attitudes and expectations, to economical systems and to political beliefs as well as to the educational system.

Activity 9.3 Vocational versus Academic?

Consider the further study choices that a young person will be expected to make at the age of 14, which will include the decision to take either Diplomas, GCSEs or some combination of both. What factors might influence these choices? How much do you agree that the routes outlined here will mean that there will be an appropriate and engaging option for all 14–19 year olds?

Government reforms of secondary education intent on providing a vocational pathway for less academic pupils may be in danger of ignoring the complexity of the interactions between pedagogy, policy and individuals. There is clearly much more at stake than a simple divide between academic and vocational routes. There are, however, encouraging indications that recent initiatives may go at least some way to restore the balance of the original Tomlinson proposals (Curtis, 2007), but this process is undoubtedly fraught with contradictory ideologies and unlikely to be straightforward. Arguably, a focus on lively teaching, engagement and practical activities, together with good differentiation as opposed to 'tinkering on a massive and expensive scale' (Hodgson and Spours, 2005: 4) may be equally effective in stemming the tide of disaffection.

Joined up thinking?

This chapter has explored disaffection with education within the wider context of social and cultural changes in our society which has effectively resulted in a body of the population who have been excluded from the process of learning and the production of knowledge, which, as Hayton (2004: 221) discusses 'has always been at the heart of how societies reproduce themselves'. Because of the complex inter-related nature of the factors involved, countering disaffection within school has to be as much about tackling social, economical and political issues as it is about changing educational systems and structures. There is now a broad consensus of agreement (Prichard and Williams, 2007; Riley and Docking, 2004) that a multi-agency approach that places schools in the centre, facilitating communication between parents, professionals and pupils is most likely to be effective. If schools are central to this approach, however, then the needs of pupils themselves must surely be at the heart. Strategies that will successfully tackle disaffection, in the widest sense, will be fully inclusive and will engage pupils in the process of gaining an education and through this to gaining recognition within society. Although the current emphasis on high standards, arguably at the expense of the individual, places schools in a difficult position; some schools are undoubtedly better at maintaining the balance between academic and pastoral and despite difficult pupils are more inclusive in their approach (Parsons, 2003: 181). A number of studies, demonstrate that such inclusive schools typically have staff prepared to invest in their pupils by forming positive relationships based on respect, humour and consistency.

As Kinder suggests, when examining how young people's attitudes can be turned around:

> [It] is important to stress that each of these pupil's recovery statements was underpinned by some form of intensive and *individualized* support from their school or off-site unit. The focus of that support had provided alternative curriculum experiences or leaning contexts and/or pastoral work for behavioural or emotional problems. As a conclusion for solutions to disaffection, this suggests that there are considerable resource implications in any serious attempt to address pupil's disengagement from school, and yet, when such resources are available, the dedication and skill of educational professionals can produce highly positive results. (Kinder, 1996: 30) [my italics]

Summary

- Transition to adult status in the UK society is far less predictable than in previous decades.
- Young people from lower socio-economic backgrounds are disproportionally exposed to higher levels of risk and restricted choices concerning their future.
- Pupils at risk of disaffection cite poor relationships with teachers as central to their engagement.
- Exclusion figures mask a worrying high level of informal and unofficial exclusion, particularly among girls.
- Curriculum focused strategies for reducing disaffection need to be considered alongside wider social, socio-economic and policy issues.

References

BBC News, 2006 available at http://news.bbc.co.uk/1hi/education/2781525.stn

Bailey, R (2005) *Challenging Disaffection: Best Practice and the Management of Disaffection*. London: ESRC

Boaler et al. (2000) 'Students' experiences of ability grouping – disaffection, polarization and the construction of failure', *British Educational Research Journal*, 26(5), 631–48

Beck, U (1992) *Risk Society: Towards a New Modernity*. London: Sage

Bunting, M (2007) 'Yes, we have failed Rhys Jones, but we have also failed his killer', *Guardian*, 27 August, Manchester

Coles, B (1995) *Youth and Social Policy*. London: UCL

Cullingford, C and Oliver, P (eds) (2001) *The National Curriculum and its Effects*. Aldershot: Ashgate Publishing

Curtis, P (2007) Balls launches first diplomas to rival 'A' levels and GCSES', *Guardian* Manchester

DfEE (1999) (Department for Education and Employment) 'Social inclusion, pupil support', Circular 10/99 London: Social Inclusion Unit, the Department of Health and the Home Office

DfES (2004b) (Department for Education and Science) '14–19 curriculum and qualifications reform'. Final report of the working group on 14–19 reform. London: DfES

DfES (2005) (Department for Education and Science) '14–19 Education and skills', London: DfES

DfES (2007) (Department for education and science) 'Raising expectations: staying in education and training post 16', London: DfES

Docking, J (1990) *Education and Alienation in the Junior School*. London: Falmer Press

Furlong, A and Cartmel, F (2007) 'Young people and social change: new perspectives', Berkshire: Open University Press

Giddens, A (1991) *Modernity and Self-identity. Self and Society in the Late Modern Age*. Oxford: Polity

Gordon, A (2001) 'School exclusions in England: children's voices and adult solutions?' *Educational Studies*, 27(1), 70–85

Green, A (1991) 'The reform of post 16 education and training', Post 16 Education Working Paper No. 11. London: Institute of Education, University of London

Hayton, A (ed.) (1999) *Tackling Disaffection and Social Exclusion: Educational Perspectives and Policies*. London: Kogan Page

Hendrick, H (1997) *Children, Childhood and English Society, 1880–1990*. Cambridge: Cambridge University Press

Hendry, L B, Shucksmith, J, Love, J G and Glendinning, A (1993) *Young People's Leisure and Lifestyles*. London: Routledge

Hidi, S and Harackiewicz, J M (2000) 'Motivating the academically unmotivated: a critical issue for the 21st century', *Review of Educational Research*, 70, 151–79

Hodgson, A and Spours, K (2005) 'Building a strong 14–19 phase in England? The Government's white paper in its wider system context', Nuffield Review of 14–19 Education and Training Discussion Paper 35

Keys, W, Harris, S and Fernandes, C (1995) *Attitudes to School of Op Primary and First Year Secondary Pupils*. Slough: NFER

Kiernan, K E (1992) 'The impact of family disruption on transitions made in young adult life', *Population Studies*, 46, 213–34

Kinder, K, Wakefield, A and Wilkin, A (1996) *Talking Back: Pupil Views on Disaffection*. Slough: NFER

Klein, N (2000) *No Logo*. London: Flamingo

Kramer, R (1991) *Education School Follies: The Mis-Education of America's Teachers*. New York: Free Press

MacDonald, R and Marsh, J (2006) *Disconnected Youth: Growing Up in Britain's Poor Neighbourhoods*. London: Palgrave

McDowell, L (2003) *Redundant Masculinities? Employment Changes and White Working Class Youth*. London: Blackwell

Muijs, D (1997) 'Self perception and performance. Predictors of academic achievement and academic self concept: a longitudinal perspective', *British Journal of Educational Psychology*, 67, 265–77

Munn, P and Lloyd, G (2005) 'Exclusion and excluded pupils', *British Educational Research Journal*, 31(2), 205–21

New Policy Institute (2006) 'Girls and school exclusion', Available at: www.npi.org.uk/summ%20girls%20exclusion.htm

Ofsted (1998) 'Work related aspects of the curriculum in secondary schools', London: HMSO

Parsons, C (1999) 'School exclusions in the UK: numbers, trends and variations', in Topping, K and Maloney, S (eds) (2005) *Reader in Inclusive Education*. Abingdon: RoutledgeFalmer

Parsons, C (2005) 'School exclusion: the will to punish', *British Journal of Education Studies*, 53(2), 180–211

Pavey, S and Visser, J (2003) 'Primary exclusions: are they rising?' *British Journal of Special Education*, 30(4), 180–86

Prichard, C, and Williams, R (2006) 'Breaking the cycle of educational alienation: a multi agency approach', Maidenhead: Open University Press

Raffe, D (2003) 'Young people not in education, employment or training: evidence from the Scottish School Leavers survey', CES Special briefing No. 29, Edinburgh: Centre for Educational Sociology, University of Edinburgh

Reid, K (2002) 'Mentoring with disaffected pupils', *Mentoring and Training*, 10(2), 153–70

Reid, K (2005) 'School absenteesism and truancy', in Topping, K and Maloney, S (eds) (2005) *Reader in Inclusive Education*. Abingdon: RoutledgeFalmer

Riddell, M (2007) 'Don't seek revenge on violent gangs. Take responsibility', *The Observer*, 26 August

Riley, K (2002) 'Working with disaffected students: why students lose interest in school and what we can do about it', London: Paul Chapman

Riley, K and Docking, J (2004) 'Voices of disaffected pupils: implications for policy and practice', *British Journal of Educational Studies*, 52(2), 166–79

Roberts, K (1995) *Youth and Employment in Modern Britain*. Oxford: Open University Press

Ross, C E and Broh, B A (2000) 'The roles of self esteem and the sense of personal control in the academic achievement process', *Sociology of Education*, 73, 270–84

Rutter, M and Smith, D J (eds) (1995) *Psychological Disorders in Young People. Time Trends and Their Causes*. Chichester: Wiley

Sanders, D and Hendry, L (1997) *New Perspectives on Disaffection*. London: Cassell

Smith, R (1998) *No Lessons Learnt: A Survey of School Exclusions*. London: The Children's Society

Solomon, Y and Rogers, C (2001) 'Motivational patterns in disaffected school pupils: insights from Pupil Referral Unit clients'. *British Educational Research Journal*, 27(3), 331–44

Thomas, H (2007) 'The conversation: secondary transition', in *Times Educational Supplement*, October

Topping, K and Maloney, S (eds) (2005) *Reader in Inclusive Education*. Abingdon: RoutledgeFalmer

Young, M (1993) 'A curriculum for the 21st Century? Towards a new basis for overcoming academic/vocational divisions', *British Journal of Educational Studies*, 41(3), 203–22

Further reading

Evans, G (2006) *Educational Failure and Working Class White Children in Britain*. London: Palgrave

Kendal, S and Kinder, K (2005) 'Reclaiming those disengaged from education and learning: a European perspective', NFER publications. Ref NRE

Moore, R (2004) *Education and Society: Issues and Explanations in the Sociology of Education*. Cambridge: Polity Press

Newburn, T, Shiner, M and Young, T (2005) *Dealing with Disaffection: Young People, Mentoring and Social Exclusion*. London: Willan Publishers

Useful websites

publications.teachernet.gov.uk/default.aspx?PageFunction=productdetails&PageMode=publications&ProductId =Cm+7065& – This website contains a host of relevant and useful publications including the Department for Education and Skills (DfES) (2007) publication: *Raising expectations: staying in education and training post 16.*

Useful internet search terms

transition stages

risk and choice

disaffected pupils

motivation and attribution theories

exclusion

vocational education

curriculum initiatives

Listening to Pupils' Voices
Margaret Wood

Introduction

This chapter will begin by examining the rationale and principles behind the importance of a commitment to understanding and taking seriously the views of young people and why it matters that they have a voice in decision-making. It will draw on practical approaches in schools to analyse and reflect on how these principles are applied in practice. International dimensions are included and these provide a broader context and wider global view.

Background and development of the policy context

This chapter will consider why it is important to listen to the voices of children and young people and to involve them in decision-making. In the humorous children's story book 'Not now Bernard' by McKee (1998), Bernard's parents provide readers with an example of adults who do not appear to attach a sense of importance to what Bernard has to say. The response received, 'Not now Bernard' which becomes a mantra repeated by his parents who ignore Bernard's calls for their attention, provides an example of adults who fail to take children's ideas seriously. In another well-known story the six-year-old child's view of the need for forbearance can be seen when adults misinterpret children's meanings. This idea is apparent when the child's picture of a scary boa constrictor swallowing an elephant was misunderstood by the grown-ups and seen from their perspective as something entirely different, namely a hat, and therefore not frightening at all. Consequently, it was necessary for the child to draw a second picture, so that it could be clearly seen by the grown ups who 'always need to have things explained' (Saint-Exupery, 1974).

In Victorian times the maxim that children should be 'seen and not heard' conveyed the view that adults know best. In contrast to this attitude of adult disinterest in and disregard for the views and voices of children, there is now a growing recognition of the importance of children and young people's participation in decision-making, not only in the United Kingdom but in other countries too. The United Nations Convention on the Rights of the Child (1989) recognizes the human rights of children and provides a set of global principles of rights to which children are entitled:

> The UN Convention on the Rights of the Child, which formally and explicitly acknowledges these rights of children for the first time in international law, also introduces an additional dimension to the status of children by recognizing that children are subjects of rights, rather than merely recipients of adult protection, and that those rights demand that children themselves are entitled to be heard. (Lansdown, 2001: 1)

Article 12 enshrines the right to be listened to and for children's views to be given 'due weight'. Lansdown (2001: 2) notes that this brings in 'a radical and profound challenge to traditional attitudes, which assume that children should be seen and not heard' and we might suggest that with this comes a new outlook on the importance and status of the views of the child.

Fielding (2006: 299) suggests that there is growing evidence from countries in Australasia, North America and the United Kingdom of a trend for governments to position consultation with young people about their experience of schooling as central rather than peripheral. Giving young people a voice and listening to what they have to say, for example through School Councils, is increasingly seen as fundamental to democratizing schools (Savage and Wood, 2006) and the Office for Standards in Education requires, as part of the inspection process, that Inspectors 'take opportunities to talk with groups of pupils, for example year group representatives, the school council or other pupils' forum' (OFSTED, 2005: 12). A main feature of inspection is the emphasis now placed on school improvement and the key role of school self-evaluation including opportunities for input from pupils as well as other stakeholders (OFSTED, 2005: 4). Indeed, it makes sense to give a voice to children and young people, as key stakeholders in a school, when it comes to gathering data for school improvement:

> The main stakeholders in a school – if we define a stakeholder as someone having a stake in the school's success – are of course those who live and work in the school itself. So the pupils have a principal claim to attention. Indeed, the literature of school improvement and effectiveness is

replete with encouragement to involve pupils in decisions about their work and the running of the school. (Brighouse and Woods, 1999: 150)

Taking seriously the role of children and young people in making decisions about matters directly related to their experiences and impacting on their lives is part of the policy context. It is given expression, for example, in the rationale behind the creation of posts such as a Children's Rights Director for England and Children's Commissioner, and is fundamental to 'Every Child Matters'. This commitment to finding out what children and young people think about their experiences is seen as part of what is described as a growing culture of participation, with insights and ideas from the younger generation recognized as valuable in potentially shaping services and policies which affect their lives and others in the community (Halsey et al., 2006: 5). Children and young people have a unique perspective to bring and the awareness of the necessity of listening to these voices to gain different insights and interpretations is a crucial idea. Kellett (2005: 3) has noted that 'Children ask different questions, have different priorities and concerns and see the world through different eyes'.

The literature on managing educational change abounds with examples of change that has not been successfully sustained often because the commitment of those involved had not been secured. Any educational enterprise needs stakeholders to have opportunities to shape and develop the changes for successful implementation and sustainability. If the phrase 'Every child matters' means anything then it must mean that children and young people are seen as people within the school community whose opinions matter and whose voices must be heard and taken seriously if education is to be personalized to their needs. Fullan (2001: 151) reminds us that

Students, even little ones, are people too. Unless they have some meaningful (to them) role in the enterprise, most educational change, indeed most education, will fail. I ask the reader not to think of students as running the school, but to entertain the following question: What would happen if we treated the student as someone whose opinion mattered in the introduction and implementation of reform in schools?

Consulting and involving young people is a key aspect of Every Child Matters (DfES, 2004) and the five outcomes for every child now form a national framework for children's services. These five outcomes are

- being healthy
- staying safe
- enjoying and achieving
- making a positive contribution
- economic wellbeing

The principle of 'involving children, young people and carers in service design and delivery and in decisions that affect them' (DfES, 2005: 6) is a key part of the rationale for service provision for children and young people from birth to age 19 years. The Every Child Matters framework and the Children Act (2004) are some of the key drivers behind the appointment of Local Authority Directors of Children's Services and the creation of integrated Children's Services Directorates. Charged with making more effective partnerships between all agencies working for children in a local area, local authorities are developing children and young people's participation and engagement in planning, delivery and evaluation of services. This is occurring through formal bodies such as Youth Councils and Youth Parliaments and less formal events such as opportunities to engage and involve children and young people across the range of backgrounds and communities represented in a local area.

The rationale for embracing engagement and participation in this way is threefold:

i) it will empower young people and contribute to the development of skills and attitudes required for active citizenship
ii) it will improve the quality and effectiveness of services for children and young people
iii) it will make a significant contribution to strengthening a democratic society in which all citizens play an active positive role

As mentioned above, a central role in making sure that children and young people's voices are heard is that given to the Children's Commissioner for England who will 'pay particular attention to gathering and putting forward the views of the most vulnerable children and young people in society, and will promote their involvement in the work of organizations whose decisions and actions affect them'. www.everychildmatters.gov.uk/aims

As part of its assessment of the effectiveness of Children's Services, the Office for Standards in Education (OFSTED) has instituted an annual national survey of children and young people's views (Tellus2 Survey) which forms part of the evidence for inspection of local authorities and their partners.

Activity 10.1 What Are Younger Children's Views on the 5 Outcomes?

Read about what children think of these 5 outcomes in a report based on the views of children from across the country, mostly aged up to 12 years. The data was gathered from the children who attended a national children's conference held in 2005 for this purpose. They were asked whether or not they agreed that the Government's 5 outcomes are all important to children. The report is entitled 'Younger Children's Views on 'Every Child Matters' from the 2005 Children's Rights National Event for children aged 12 and under.' This is an opportunity to hear what this age group think. You can download the report from the Commission for Social Care Inspection Children's website at www.rights4me.org where you will find it in the Reports Archive section of the 'Be Heard' area of the website.

Applying a model of participation to thinking about practice

Something of the rationale underpinning a commitment to listen to the voices of children and young people has been discussed above. This section will consider consultation and participation in a range of contexts, both in this country and internationally. For example, a survey of the opinions of over 10,000 children across East Asia and the Pacific region was conducted to uncover their views on a range of issues shaping their lives. This has provided valuable data which has the potential to inform dialogue between children and those whose decisions and actions affect their lives (UNICEF, 2001a: 12). This will be referred to again below.

The Ladder of Young People's Participation (Hart, 1992) provides a useful framework to help us to reflect on the scope for participation, conceptualized as the rungs on a ladder. The rungs reflect the extent to which young people actually are involved and engaged. The lower three rungs are non-participation. The other rungs describe different degrees of participation (Figure 10.1).

Activity 10.2 Applying Hart's Ladder

Read the following summary of the George Mitchell Community School's 'Making Learning Better' scheme, adapted and condensed from an article which appeared in an issue of the Secondary Headship publication. Reflect on this example, drawing on Hart's framework to inform your thinking about this school's approach to student voice.

Reflect on Hart's framework and apply it to your thinking about schools or education settings with which you are familiar. Identify examples of opportunities in these schools and settings for children and young people to be consulted and to have an active role in sharing in decision-making.

An example of good practice: making learning better – listening to pupil voice at George Mitchell Community School (adapted from Savage and Wood, 2006)

George Mitchell Community School (GMCS) is in the London Borough of Waltham Forest. Its Making Learning Better (MLB) approach to student voice was noted by the OFSTED, as an outstanding feature. This approach at the school has received national media coverage which has in turn generated interest from other schools eager to learn from this experience.

Central to the MLB approach at GMCS are the learning consultants – students who are trained to carry out regular lesson observations and to offer feedback to teachers on how

Rung 8	Child-initiated shared decision-making with adults	Degrees of participation
Rung 7	Child-initiated and led	
Rung 6	Adult-initiated, shared decisions with children	
Rung 5	Consulted and informed	
Rung 4	Assigned but informed	
Rung 3	Tokenism*	Non-participation
Rung 2	Decoration*	
Rung 1	Manipulation*	

* Rungs 1-3 represent non-participation

Figure 10.1 Children's participation from tokenism to citizenship.
Source: UNICEF Adapted from Hart, R (1992)

to make learning better in the classroom. Both staff and students are seen as key sources of knowledge about learning. The learning consultants can be viewed as staff developers who contribute to the development of a shared conversation about learning in the school. The young people, as learning consultants in MLB play an important part in developing knowledge and understanding about pedagogy and practice through their evaluations of the quality of the learning experiences and their feedback to staff.

The young people involved in MLB are trained for their role as learning consultants and an important part of this role is to question how effective their lessons have been. The training is therefore in itself a valuable lesson in developing key transferable skills of questioning, problem-solving, critical thinking and observation skills, as well as interpersonal skills such as giving feedback. They develop the skills of training peers to act as learning consultants at other schools, they give presentations about the scheme and through all this they gain confidence. As one Year 10 learning consultant remarked: 'We have learned how to talk to teachers on a more professional level'. Another learning consultant from the same year added 'and they listen to us'.

The learning consultant receives a copy of the teacher's lesson plan several days before the class they are to observe and, following the observation, feedback is given to the teacher.

Any student can apply to become a learning consultant. They are encouraged to do so based on how much they enjoy the subject, as this would seem to give them the strongest motivation to want to improve the way it is taught. Learning consultants come from across the age and ability range. The school was keen from the outset that being a learning consultant should *not* be the exclusive domain of the more gifted student. Staff are encouraged to gain immediate feedback at the end of their lessons by asking pupils for their views in response to the question 'How could that lesson have been better?' This is powerful as it is instant, direct and provides valuable data for teachers to evaluate their lessons.

The learning consultants affirm that MLB changes the learning environment and they report that their relationship with teachers is good: 'There's more respect. They listen.'

So how genuine a 'voice' do the students have? The school is keen to avoid tokenistic gestures and to ensure that what has been put in place is based on shared values. This is a strategy for quality enhancement by sharing views and explanations of what works in the classroom. Student voice is key to this. MLB is based on a passionately held belief that only by harnessing the views of learners can truly personalized learning be guaranteed. The whole personalized learning agenda is perhaps most central of all to the future evolution of secondary education in this country, but how can you personalize the learning without learning from the person at its core?

Engaging students as active researchers

A second example of Good Practice:
A 'voice' through research – Students As Researchers (STARS)
(adapted from Lucas and Wood, 2007)

Giving young people a voice in these ways empowers them as active citizens to share responsibility for decision-making. Another example of promoting active citizenship and giving young people a voice is through engaging them in planning and conducting their own research enquiries. Traditionally, research has been thought of as something planned and carried out by adults. This may have been based on assumptions that research is either too hard for children and young people, or that they lack the skills and maturity needed. Kellett (2005) has shown how these barriers can be overcome and how children can engage as active researchers without any dilution of the research process. Kellett's concern is with teaching the research process to children. As well as huge learning benefits, research is an important way in which children can create their own original knowledge.

> A vast amount of new knowledge is generated by research and much knowledge is also affirmed or discredited by research. One of these bodies of knowledge is about children and childhood, yet it has been constructed almost entirely by adults. . . . Children are acknowledged as experts on their own lives (Alderson, 2000; Mayall, 2000; Christensen and Prout 2002) and if adults genuinely want to understand children and childhood, better ways to seek out child perspective and unlock child voice must be sought. (Kellett, 2005: 2)

Kellett maintains that by empowering children as active researchers, important original knowledge is generated which can inform our understanding about childhood and children's lives. This is not a perspective on children's lives as seen and interpreted through an adult lens. It is an understanding based on children's own original knowledge which is gained through their own research enquiries. This idea of creating original and new knowledge which is uniquely their own is indicated in the name which one of Kellett's groups of young researchers adopted. This was the 'Original Knowledge' club and therefore known as the 'O.K.' club. During a particular year 9 young researchers in the next scenario made the same point when commenting that 'young adults have different views and perspectives on things'. An example of giving young people a voice through research is the Students as Researchers (STARS) work at Deptford Green secondary school in the London borough of Lewisham. The STARS work disproves the notion that research is too hard for children and that it is therefore best left to adults. STARS engages young people as active researchers with a voice in the school and the community and the potential to influence change.

STARS is a vehicle for student voice, promoted within Citizenship as a means of researching and taking forward students' ideas. The young people's research projects often have a focus on 'change-action', seeking to make a difference by influencing change in the school and the community.

In terms of student voice, this has not been tokenistic. The young researchers have, through their research investigations, prompted and initiated changes. For example, through their research investigations they have

- Investigated and reported on leisure facilities in the area. Their feedback to adults from the community, including a representative from the local council, was followed by a major financial investment by the council into developing leisure facilities in the local park.
- organized a recycling scheme in school
- investigated problems with the toilets and heating problems in the sports hall and got these fixed
- researched, designed and implemented change to three classrooms
- Been the catalyst for a road improvement scheme to include pedestrian crossings near the school and netting put in place by two different railway network companies to prevent birds perching above the pavement which passed below a railway bridge. The result of these change-actions is that travel between the two sites is a safer and far more pleasant experience for students.

To make their findings available to a wider audience the young researchers have made presentations to different audiences including the local police, peers, staff at the school, school governors, local councillors, local authority representatives and the MP.

The question posed by Fullan (2001: 151) asked: 'What would happen if we treated the student as someone whose opinion mattered in the introduction and implementation of reform in schools?' At Deptford Green student research provided important data for school improvement and self-evaluation. For example, the STARS research into the causes of poor behaviour and their recommendations for how this might be improved were based on data they collected through lesson observations and interviews conducted with staff and peers. There were some real insights here into behaviour management and a booklet resulted from this which offered 'Tips on attitude of teachers from a pupil's point of view':

'We like it when teachers are firm but funny.'
'We don't like it when teachers shout at us for no reasons and for the simplest thing.'

'We don't like the activities and fun parts to take place all at once. Like the end or the start, we like it to be spread out so pupils don't get bored.'

'Teachers should try and get everyone involved in the activities – the teacher should also get involved!' A number of suggestions followed for strategies to encourage pupils to get more involved in learning.

Here the voices of young people have been heard by a school which is listening, taking their views seriously and building this data into evaluation and review to promote improvement. Here is active citizenship embodied as young people are thinking and acting responsibly and playing a key part in the life of the school community. They are enquiring into issues and topics of importance to them and expressing opinions based on their research evidence.

The Children's Research Centre website at the Open University where Dr Kellett is the Director can be accessed at childrens-research-centre.open.ac.uk/. Here you can see examples of research studies undertaken by children and young people.

Activity 10.3

There are different ways in which this kind of young researchers' programme might be provided, for example as an extracurricular activity or within areas of the curriculum such as Personal, Social and Health Education (PSHE) and Citizenship (Kellett, 2004). Kellett's research programmes have included pupils as young five year olds.

Step 1. Identify possible topics within Citizenship or PSHE where children and young people might design research projects, collect and analyse data and disseminate their findings (oral or written or both) for an audience.

Step 2. Produce a diagrammatic overview/map of all the different areas of the topic that you have chosen and then identify one specific aspect which might form the basis of an enquiry.

Step 3. Draft a possible research question for a small-scale investigation. Remember to keep the question tightly framed and focused on something very specific within your chosen topic which you want to find out about. For example, you might decide to focus on interactive learning. The young researchers at Deptford Green provide us with a model here. They wanted to make lessons more interactive: 'We were trying to make lessons interactive to get pupils engaged in the lessons, to make it better for teachers to teach and learners to learn' (Year 9 Young Researcher). First, the student researchers needed clarity about what staff and pupils understood by 'interactive learning'. They gathered data from staff and students using questionnaires and lesson observations. They reported their findings and produced a resource of practical ideas and activities which they called 'Go Interactive' available for staff to draw on when planning lessons.

Here is an example of a diagrammatic representation of different aspects of the topic of 'Making Learning Fun' (Figure 10.2). Taking the nature of work at school as an area, one aspect to focus on might be strategies to promote interactive learning in the classroom.

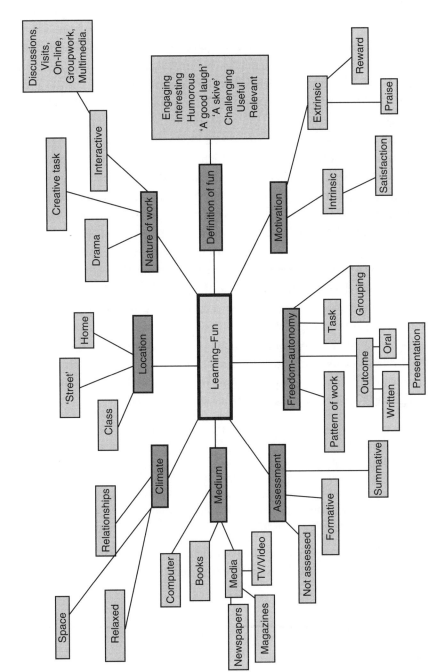

Figure 10.2 Making learning fun.

Listening to children's voices – international dimensions

Examples of structures and strategies aimed at giving children and young people a voice in matters affecting them have been considered, in this final section of the chapter children's views and opinions informing policy development in a global context will be discussed.

Here are examples of how this has worked for children and young people living in poor and disadvantaged communities where the provision of opportunities to participate as active citizens has been empowering. In Lansdown (2001: 28) writes about the Butterflies Programme of Street and Working Children which involves about 800 children who live and work on New Delhi's streets. There is a team of street educators who are central to gaining the children's trust and respect and getting them to participate in a range of activities which include non-formal education, saving schemes, recreational and health, most of which the children also have some share in planning. An important feature of the programme is the monthly Children's Council meeting to which representatives bring issues raised by the children so these can be aired. At these Council meetings children can discuss matters important and relevant to their lives and the principles of active citizenship seem to be embodied in this. Actions have resulted such as the organization of a Child Workers Union, a Credit Union and the Child Workers Voice. (Lansdown, 2001: 28)

This is a good example of a programme which is based on 'forming respectful relationships with the children and enabling them to participate in their own forums to identify the issues that concern them' (ibid.). The programme has empowered these children as active citizens, having experienced negative adult attitudes towards them:

> Indeed, the greatest barriers faced by the children are the negative attitudes of many adults: employers, community members and official bodies who believe that they know best and lack belief in children's capacity to participate, and the police and general public who see the children as thieves rather than individuals struggling to survive. Also, the parents of those children living at home are often reluctant to allow them to participate in the programmes. Butterflies highlights the need to educate adults, raising their awareness of the importance of respecting children's rights and acknowledging children's own active participation in the exercise of those rights (Lansdown, 2001: 28).

A key point is that this is described as an example of 'self-advocacy' which is 'a process of empowering children themselves to take action to address those issues that they see as important' (Lansdown, 2001: 26).

Activity 10.4

From the brief synopsis given here, what would you suggest might be some of the features of a programme of 'self-advocacy'? What do you suggest would be an appropriate role for adults to have?

Compare your ideas with the following characteristics:

- the issues of concern are identified by children themselves
- the role of adults is to facilitate, not lead
- the process is controlled by children (Lansdown, 2001: 27)

The UNICEF regional survey (2001a) of the views of children in the East Asia and Pacific Region involved a sample of over 10,000 children between the ages of 9 and 17 years and covered 17 countries and territories in this region. The survey wanted to provide an opportunity for children's voices to be heard on a range of many different topics such as, for instance, relationships with parents, teachers and school, the values they hold, dangers of drugs and HIV/AIDS, and feeling safe in their communities, in order to gain a better understanding of children's opinions. Driven by a desire to give children a forum through which they can be heard, an important goal of this survey was that they would not only be heard but that their views would provide a better understanding of what children think about the world they are growing up in and the issues they face. The survey therefore provides 'a glimpse into the hearts and minds of children' and data to inform and influence how future policies that affect children and young people are developed.

The aim was that the release of the survey's full results would promote even greater debate and serve to inform governments and policy-makers, as well as parents and community leaders, and encourage them to give their children more active roles in decision-making processes. (UNICEF, 2001a: 9)

Activity 10.5

Find out about the C8 Children's Forum 2005. The website tells us:

In July 2005, in the run-up to the G8 summit, young people from eight of the world's poorest countries met with young people from G8 countries. This meeting, organized by UNICEF, was called the C8 Children's Forum. Together, they produced Children for Change, a set of recommendations for the G8 leaders, calling for a better, fairer world for children everywhere. www.j8summit.com/uk/pages/5/348

Conclusion

In this chapter the role of listening to and understanding the views expressed by children and young people has been discussed, arguing that this makes good sense in terms of more informed and effective decision-making on matters affecting their lives. In terms of the

Butterflies Programme, for example, Lansdown (2001: 28) noted that

> The programme demonstrates not only that children are capable of participating and contributing towards the development and running of programmes, but also that programmes are more effective when children are directly involved.

Furthermore, taking their views seriously shows respect for children and young people and tells them that their ideas and opinions do count. The concept of 'voice' has been set within a wider policy framework and we have explored some practical examples drawn from school settings and from a wider global view, where listening to and consulting with children and young people is taken as fundamentally important to the principle of active citizenship and participation in schools and communities and wider society.

Summary/key points

- listening to and understanding the voices of children and young people is important
- involving children and young people in decision-making on matters which affect their lives is important and has been considered against the backdrop of the wider policy framework
- some practical examples of young people's participation in their schools and communities have been suggested

References

Brighouse, T and Woods, D (1999) *How to Improve Your School.* London: Routledge

Commission for Social Care Inspection (2005) 'Younger children's views on 'Every Child Matters' from the 2005 Children's Rights National Event for Children aged 12 and under', Newcastle upon Tyne: The Children's Rights Team. Available at: www.rights4me.org (accessed 17 September 2007)

Department for Education and Skills (2004) 'Every child matters: change for children in schools', Nottingham: DfES Publications

Department for Education and Skills (2005) 'Common core of skills ad knowledge for the children's workforce', Nottingham: DfES Publications

Fielding, M (2006) 'Leadership, radical student engagement and the necessity of person-centred education', *International Journal of Leadership in Education,* 9(4) 299–313

Fullan, M (2001) *The New Meaning of Educational Change.* London: RoutledgeFalmer & Teachers College Press

Halsey, K, Murfield, J, Harland, J and Lord, P (2006) *The Voice of Young People: an engine for improvement? Scoping the evidence.* Slough: National Foundation for Educational Research

Hart, R (1992) 'Children's participation from tokenism to citizenship', Florence: UNICEF Innocenti Research Centre www.unicef-irc.org/publications/pdf/childrens_participation.pdf (accessed 19 January 2008)

Kellett, M (2005) *How to Develop Children as Researchers.* London: Paul Chapman

Kellett, M (2004) 'The research challenge', in Teaching Thinking and Creativity. Summer 2004 www.teachingthinking.com (accessed 21 September 2007)

Lansdown, G (2001) 'Promoting children's participation in democratic decision-making', Florence: UNICEF Innocenti Research Centre www.unicef-icdc.org/publications/pdf/insight6.pdf (accessed 22 September 2007)

Lucas, D and Wood, M (2007) *Students as Researchers: Making a Difference at Deptford Green Secondary School. Secondary Headship*

McKee, D (1998) *Not Now Bernard*. Harlow: Longman

Morgan, R (2005) *Younger Children's Views on "Every Child Matters"*. Newcastle upon Tyne: Commission for Social Care Inspection

Office for Standards in Education (2005) 'Framework 2005: Framework for the Inspection of Schools in England from September 2005', London: OFSTED. www.ofsted.gov.uk (accessed 29 September 2007)

Saint-Exupery, A (1974) *The Little Prince*. London: Pan Books

Savage, M and Wood, M (2006) *Making Learning Better: Listening to Pupil Voice*. Secondary Headship Issue 48

United Nations Children's Fund (2001a) Speaking Out! Voices of children and adolescents in East Asia and the Pacific. Bangkok: UNICEF

United Nations Children's Fund (2001b) Young Voices: Opinion Survey of Children and Young People in Europe and Central Asia. Geneva: United Nations Children's Fund

Further reading

Department for Children, Schools and Families (2008) 'Working together. Listening to the voices of children and young people', Available at: www.teachernet.gov.uk/publications

Pulley, H and Jagger, L (2006) '. . . and the pupil said. Learning from pupil voice to guide a more personalized approach to learning and teaching', Available at: www.ncsl.org.uk

Useful websites

www.cfbt.com/evidenceforeducation/Default.aspx?page=338 – Evidence for Education CfBT Education Trust website.

The National Foundation for Educational Research (2006) undertook a literature review of the impact of the voice of young people in education and the report was entitled 'The voice of young people: an engine for improvement? Scoping the evidence.' You can download a summary of this literature review or the full report from the CfBT Education Trust website.

www.childrens-research-centre.open.ac.uk – The website of the Children's Research Centre based at the Open University.

www.everychildmatters.gov.uk/ – Department for Children, Schools and Families website about Every Child Matters.

www.oxfam.org.uk/coolplanet/kidsweb – Oxfam Cool Planet website Oxfam GB's website for children and teachers.

www.unicef.org/ – The United Nations Children's Fund. UNICEF works internationally for children's rights.

www.unicef-irc.org/ – UNICEF Innocenti Research Centre.

www.unicef.org/voy/ – The Voices of Youth area of the UNICEF website.

Useful internet search terms

participation

pupil voice

young researchers
active citizenship
student researchers
listening to children and young people
children and decision-making

Education Beyond Schools

Les Hankin

11

Introduction

Education beyond schools is generally taken to refer to sectors of learning that fall beyond the stages of compulsory education. These include further education, higher education, workplace learning and the whole vast arena of adult learning in formal and informal, social and cultural settings. The problems of describing this part of the educational landscape, with its seemingly limitless contours, say much about the shifting concept of education and its place in all our lives.

Not so long ago it was clear what Education was for. It was about schooling and it was about youth. There were few opportunities for many young people to progress beyond or outside the four high walls of the school. That picture has changed out of all recognition. Indeed one of the drivers in the resurgence of Education Studies as an essential subject in its own right is the growing recognition of governments that education must go beyond schools. This principle, known by the shorthand term lifelong learning, is now essential to the rhetoric of formal educational policy and practice as well as being an everyday informal reality for all of us. The United Kingdom now has its own minister for lifelong learning, located in the Department for Innovation, Universities and Skills and charged with making learning-without-limits an opportunity for all.

Activity 11.1

Visit the DIUS website and find out about the roles and responsibilities of this minister – www.dius. gov.uk/

Lifelong learning is a worldwide phenomenon of such power that the International Commission on Education for the Twenty-first century, reporting to UNESCO, enshrines the belief in education throughout life as the principle organizing factor for the future. It must rest upon four pillars: learning to know, learning to do, learning to live together and learning to be (Delors et al., 2007). Such formulations place great expectations on each of us as learners, not only that we will develop self-reliance and skills, but that we will become socially mobile and economically active while living virtuously and in harmony in an increasingly precarious world. They also demand that every one of us should recognize each event in our lives as a learning opportunity and that "every individual must be in a position to keep learning throughout [their] life" (Faure, 1972: 181).

Survival

The increasing complexity of the world, with the demands it makes on our autonomy, creativity and ability to work cooperatively, requires a commitment from each of us to learn again and anew across our lifespan (Aspin 2007). With our useful working lives expanding, schools are no longer sufficient for this great task and the efforts being made to extend students' time in formal education, as well as to energize informal education, are to do not just with economic survival but also with fairness, as countries transform themselves into knowledge-based economies. What nation would not want a civilized, inclusive society, with a skilled workforce? But which is the priority?

The economic argument is pressing and the need for national workforce planning may never have been greater. A demographic time-bomb can be heard ticking, so that one day soon there may be more retired people than the working population can support. The fear of such imbalances has been with us for hundreds of years (Midwinter, 2004) but there is growing evidence that a skills crisis looms in the United Kingdom, with not enough young people coming through to take over all the high-skill jobs of the baby boomer generation as it fades into the sunset. The United Kingdom's potential to meet its future skills-needs trails behind its neighbours despite prodigious efforts to form a high-skills economy behind an expansion of higher education (Leitch, 2006). This is in a country where one in five people cannot use the yellow pages to find a plumber and where the number of young people Not in Education, Employment or Training (NEETs) is said to have grown by 15 per cent since the turn of this century.

Activity 11.2

Visit the poverty website (www.poverty.org.uk/18/index.shtml) for a visual sense of NEET. You will find links there to relevant government policies. In particular, follow the link to the report for the Department for Children, Schools and Families entitled Young people not in education, employment or training: evidence from the Education Maintenance Allowance Database. Read this.

The nature of work is changing profoundly as we move away from the industrial age. Fewer people are needed in the manufacturing and production sectors. New knowledge-based industries demand high added-value capability in IT communication and higher literacy, as well as problem-solving and interpersonal skills. Futurologists argue that there will also be a huge demand for unskilled workers and that this will exacerbate inequalities and tensions between the skilled and unskilled (Dryden and Vos, 2005). The nature of jobs is changing: they are becoming less lifelong and more episodic and short-term, uncoupled from single-career security and pensions. What is generally agreed is that now more than ever learning enhances earnings and job prospects. As well as this, all these fundamental shifts in what constitutes a 'working life' require us to rethink the place of employment in our lives and the extent to which it can still satisfy our psychological and emotional needs as well as our prosperity.

The reach of the learning society

There seems little doubt among policy-makers in the United Kingdom and elsewhere that learning beyond school helps maintain the social fabric all the way from the cradle to the grave. Sure Start runs programmes designed to educate parents and carers in the widest sense. Adult education is at the heart of the national mental-health strategy. The neighbourhood renewal strategy sees continued learning as essential for communities fighting to overcome social exclusion. Taking part in learning is claimed to increase racial tolerance, give you a better chance of giving up smoking, and prolong your active life in retirement, delaying the so-called 'fourth age' of dependence. Research by such bodies as the

Wider Benefits of Learning research centre at London University gives substance to these claims.

The government has recognized lifelong learning as 'a fundamental shift from a "once in a lifetime" approach . . . to one of educational progression linked to a process of continuous personal and professional development' (White Paper on Higher Education, 2003). Increasingly significant is the concept of 'flexible retirement'. This allows the employee to negotiate the age and length of time they take to retire as well as the nature and intensity of the work they do up to that point. It is said to remove the 'cliff edge', the trauma of going from full to no employment overnight. As a strategic response to demographic change, it gives them time to pass on their 'corporate knowledge' to succeeding generations as well as dignifying their transition to a productive and learning 'third age'.

Those school walls, like so many other barriers, have been dissolved by the global information age and the relentless internet revolution of the digital society. All these now taken-for-granted advances mark a paradigm shift in the learning process and in access to knowledge, which can be picked up instantly at the point of need. Knowledge is said to have changed as a construct. No longer absolute, stable and permanent, it has become like the web on which it proliferates: experimental, problem-orientated and open to challenge and change. As a consequence, learning can no longer be driven by old forms of teaching, as it has become more student-centred, self-directed and highly differentiated to individual needs, learning styles and pace. It has formed no less than a 'new educational order' (Field, 2006).

The internet has emerged at just the right historical moment, since the resources are not there to lifelong-teach the lifelong-taught in any formal sense. It has shifted the focus from the teacher to the learner, who can actively customize content to their needs. They can search for high-quality training opportunities often linked to occupational standards and national qualifications and, by learning anywhere where they can find an internet connection, they can overcome the barriers of cash and time poverty, childcare costs and employment downtime.

A brief historical outline of developments

The phenomenon of learning beyond school has changed considerably as national, international and individual needs have transformed its characteristics and rationale. It rests on a long tradition of learning for self-realization and betterment and to improve the quality of people's lives. Many great thinkers have taught themselves of course, autodidacts who have relied on the growing wonders of libraries, books and now the Net to furnish their minds. Adult groups emerged such as the Workers' Educational Association. Founded early in the twentieth century to help people realize their full potential in a democratic society through learning, it has a particular concern for 'those who have missed out on education' and is now the largest voluntary provider of adult education (WEA, 2007).

Lifelong learning in its current form has taken shape over the last half century. UNESCO's commitment to 'lifelong education', as long ago as 1965, was heralded as 'the master concept for educational policies in the years to come for both developed and developing countries'

(Faure et al., 1972: 182). This came at a time when formal schooling was under sustained critique from influential thinkers who judged the institution to be irrelevant, divisive, 'dead' (Illich, 1970; Reimer, 1971).

An OECD report of 1973 argued for radical change in the distribution of educational opportunities to overcome disconnections between education and the world of work as well as deep and troubling concerns about efficiency and morale in secondary education systems. The report urged governments not to strive to extend the initial period of schooling but to set up educational patterns that would enable adults to return periodically to learning throughout their lifetimes. Such a remodelling, which might have overcome intergenerational injustice, was not adopted (Istance et al., 2002). Instead all countries opted to delay young people's transition to working life by retaining them for longer in the formal system. OECD's comparative performance indicators show that over half of high school graduates in its member countries go on to higher education at some point, against a figure of just one in ten less than half a century ago. The United Kingdom now requires all young people to have educational opportunities up to the age of 18 and has set a target for 50 per cent to experience an expanded higher education system. This is its so-called Widening Participation strategy.

Labour had come to power at the end of the twentieth century propelled by a belief that education could be transformative: it had to be about more than learning for work for all except the favoured few. It needed to help people enrich their lives and those of their communities, to help them help their children and to prolong their purposeful active lives. It must address the intractable issues of the age, such as poorly educated people trapped on the minimum wage, teenage mothers, the pervasive discrimination of the learning disabled, the difficulties of minority ethnic groups who may need language skills to participate in full community life and to gain the skills needed for employability.

The government's introduction of individual learning accounts was a way of encouraging and contributing to the costs of people's education, Even as it was derailed by fraud it did uncover a huge demand for learning, as long as people could choose for themselves what, where and when they could learn. The government went further with initiatives to develop learning for adults in the poorest communities. Its Skills for Life strategy, which offers people with low skills the chance to improve them, has already given more than three million people opportunities to improve their literacy, numeracy and language skills.

The costs of these initiatives had to be met, largely by appeals to government, individuals and employers to invest more. Subsidies were offered to employers to offset training costs against a background of increasing fees, with much of the new provision financed through cuts in other areas of adult learning. All this took its toll and the Learning and Skills Council, the government body created 'to make England better skilled and more competitive', monitored declines from those heady days across further education, adult and community learning (LSC, 2007). Labour was accused of abandoning its vision for lifelong and life-wide learning for all, substituting utilitarianism, narrowing its effective support to employers and to people seeking certain qualifications.

These movements have influenced the concept of the Educated Person. This notional social archetype is expected to form the heart of society as never before, as custodian and embodiment of knowledge, values, beliefs and commitments in the new knowledge society. Such a person will increasingly be someone who has learned how to learn, and continues to learn throughout their lifetime, especially in and out of formal education (Drucker, 1993). If we accept that the Educated Person is a construct necessary for the health of society and of individuals, we must address questions about agency, culture, the negotiated nature of education and identity and the role of school and university as sites of cultural (re)production (Levinson et al., 1996).

Widening participation

As suggested above, widening access to post-compulsory education, and most particularly widening participation, has become a central plank of policy designed to make educational opportunity fairer for all. Widening participation 'for social justice and economic competitiveness', to give its full expression as set out in the government's white paper on the future of higher education (DfES, 2003), has modulated with changes in the conditions for students and persistent evidence of the intractable nature of the educational class divide. Widening participation is an attractive doctrine because it appears to reconcile the objectives of social justice, social efficiency and social mobility as it assaults the barriers to an education-based meritocracy.

Widening participation policy puts pressure on higher education institutions to widen their reach and to recruit more evenly, particularly in terms of social class and ethnic heritage, within the ambit of a learning society. Its accepted meaning covers activity aimed at creating a higher education system that includes as of right 'all who can benefit from it' (Allen and Storan, 2005: 3). It addresses deep concerns about social-class differentials in participation rates: the wealthier socio-economic classes continue to dominate university populations. Widening participation denotes action to encourage potential students from under-represented groups to contemplate and then succeed in higher education. These groups include

- low participation neighbourhoods
- black and minority ethnic communities
- lower socio-economic groups, specifically social classes 111m-V
- mature students and students progressing from Further Education routes
- disabled students
- families with little or no experience of higher education

While the number of applicants to Higher Education has increased despite the imposition of tuition fees, the least favoured groups continue to lose ground and the reach of students' academic ambition and success appears stubbornly governed by that of their parents (UCAS, 2007; HECSU, 2007). A family history of Higher Education experience appears significantly more likely to normalize it and provide moral support and encouragement for students' ambitions and aspirations.

The white paper states its concern as being to change the class bias of Higher Education and enabling students to complete their studies successfully, rather than with increasing numbers. There are ethical issues that need to be considered however.

The sentiment for widening access and participation is nearly as old as state education, but it emerged as a determinant in higher education in the post-war reforms of the 1940s, intended to treat children of all social classes equally. With the introduction of mandatory grants for higher education, social justice demanded that university entrance become an impartial, exam-driven process (Anderson, 1992). Widening participation first registers as a label for a specific strand of government policy in the debate around lifelong learning as advanced by Dearing for higher education (NCIHE, 1997) and by Kennedy and Fryer for further and continuing education in the same year.

Higher education and the knowledge society

The recent transformation of Higher Education is a phenomenon that has been experienced right across the world. Change has been forced by a set of radicalizing and interrelated pressures, including expansion of the sector ('massification'), the changing student profile, pressures from industry, increased competition and information technology capability.

Changes in the funding of institutions and their student populations have intersected with this shift from elite to mass systems of higher education, that necessarily draw from a much larger and more diversified student pool. The effects of the technology revolution in mediating knowledge to the so-called learning (or knowledge) society cannot be underestimated. To call it a knowledge society is to move universities 'absolutely centre stage', loaded with society's expectations and therefore required to anticipate, engage with and help form them (Coldstream, 2003: 4).

All these challenges and opportunities have made possible the emergence of new forms of educational institutions, many of them venerable colleges baptized anew as universities, against a background in which the shifting concept of the university and of lifelong learning are under sustained critique. Where the university might once have been immune to market pressures in its dedication to the pursuit of pure culture, Readings (1997) has famously described it as an institution in ruins, raddled by consumerist ideology and forced to produce graduates more as objects than subjects.

The higher education sector is more than ever expected to play an effective and democratizing role in the knowledge economy, redistributing as well as creating wealth, cultural resources and life opportunities. UK government policy has played on the dual themes of 'opportunity and responsibility', declared innocent of dogma, ideology and hangovers from past settlements, as a strictly meritocratic programme is forged. This derives from the all-EU Agreement of 2001 (Lisbon Strategy) which, by resolving to draw more of those within its populations into education, is perceived as integral to the mechanisms for European survival (CEU, 2001). The equation of educational attainment with economic growth is an irrefutable assumption of all governments' policy (OECD, 2004).

Problems

Among the many problems associated with such a grand social project is that it largely rules out age as one of those social categories, along with race/ethnicity, social class, sexuality and gender, where under-representation resides. The tensions between policy and individual subjectivity need also to be considered, since the right of individuals to choose and their subsequent engagement and retention are major factors. A paradox has been identified where the expansion of Higher Education may have been accompanied by a 'deepening of educational and social stratification and the emergence of new forms of inequality', as betrayed by the actual choices and movements of students into higher education (Reay et al., 2005: vii).

Changes in the general student demographic include marked increases in the proportions of female students (against male), the rise of part-time, mostly mature, entrants, and the slowly increasing participation of young people from minority ethnic backgrounds. Against these can be set a persistent under-representation of certain minority groups, those with disability, looked-after young people and those entering from vocational routes. Most obstinate is the strong negative link between socio-economic deprivation and participation. It is in the nature of Widening participation to attract a greater proportion of students with strong community and family ties, who choose not to leave home to pursue their studies and whose choice of institution is governed as much as anything by prosaic social factors such as bus routes. An impression can be gained that widening participation, along with other aspects of the social agenda promoting equality of opportunity, is entirely ethically secure because it is a good thing, legitimated through the weight of commitment shown by governments and universities. It is striking to note however how little power and voice the subjects of the grand Widening participation project are given. The expansion of access rests on the moral and practical assumption that it is inherently desirable and beneficial to the individual, hampered only by their low aspirations and achievement.

Aspiration appears however to be the province of the adult: the white paper is 'about aspiration. We must have the highest aspirations for every child whatever their talents and ability'. Young people's refusal to conform entirely to the drive to extend their formal education is usually represented as *low* aspiration whereas it might be more fairly characterized as *different* aspiration (Watts and Bridges, 2006). Corrosive labels like NEET, as used earlier in this chapter, are applied to demonstrate to such people that resistance to an economic enabling agenda is increasingly seen as culpable and inimical to society's (and the individual's) progress.

The drive for wider participation and the massification of higher education are making Higher Education a normal experience and are turning it into a rite of passage for young people as they enter adulthood and adapt to civic responsibility. In this way university becomes both norm and normative. The wider ambition on which it rests increases the responsibility of university education to offer more than the promise of a greater rate of private individual economic and social return. This has been used shamelessly to encourage school students to invest in Higher Education but it is increasingly challenged along with the accepted linkage between national levels of education and a nation's economic success (Wolf, 2002).

Challenging the learning society

The constructs 'Learning Society' and 'Knowledge Society', even the 'Learning Age', evoke visions of an open society, where development of self for the benefit of others is encouraged by policy that is enlightened, resolute and robust enough to fuse the worlds of work and learning, allowing a new consensus to emerge on the aims and purposes of education. Along with lifelong learning, these terms are contested however for the narrow link they claim between learning opportunity and social capital (Field, 2005). Both are seen as key attributes of modern societies, as they have matured from being idealized and elusive concepts of reform to become human capital-based, utilitarian models (Schuetze, 2006: 293). The most significant characteristic of lifelong learning may turn out to be that it is driven by economic imperatives, where its agenda for upskilling the workforce would be good for widening participation generally.

The prominence given to self-reliance, skills and social mobility is said to come at the expense of the wider needs of society (Edwards, 1997; Edwards et al., 2002). Some interpretations see the construct not so much as self-evident good but as social control. There may be visible signs of this effect in the phenomenon of the reluctant learner in higher education. You may well have encountered disgruntled students who feel forced to remain in institutional learning by negative incentives: the cost of not participating in university education is displacement within a labour market calibrated ever more exclusively for graduates.

More or less subtle reconstructions of lifelong learning have been interpreted as obscuring the subtext of economic compulsion, nourishment and duty through a rebranding or 'remoralisation' of it in a shift of policy emphasis (Selwyn and Gorard, 2003). Its transformative potential, at the level of civic engagement, cohesion and general quality of life, may be linked to the economic impacts for the individual and the wider community, but the social and cultural benefits often appear as secondary concerns (Brennan et al., 2006).

The sectors of learning beyond school in the United Kingdom

Lifelong Learning UK is the Sector Skills Council responsible for the professional development of all those working in community learning and development, further education, higher education, libraries, archives and information services, and work-based learning, areas traditionally used to competing with each other for limited funds.

Further Education, the sector closest to schools but seen as their very poor older cousin, has its own improvement strategy, Success for All, whose work includes pursuing teaching and learning resources for college staff developing the subjects covered by the new specialized diplomas in the 14–19 sector.

A number of agencies, such as the Learning Skills Council and the Quality Improvement Agency, work to maintain standards. Lifelong Learning UK is the new sector skills council for the learning and skills workforce.

Ufi Ltd is the government-backed lifelong learning initiative, known best for learndirect, its nationwide network of online learning and information services.

Volunteering England, which encourages and coordinate volunteering activity as civic engagement, is recognized as contributing to the lifelong learning agenda, particularly since volunteers often regard their work as a learning experience.

At the end of the spectrum is the University of the Third Age (U3A) whose founding principles are to 'assail the dogma of intellectual decline with age. For those who have learnt freedom from work, it should provide the resources to develop their intellectual and cultural lives'. A network of over five hundred autonomous U3As across the country gather in homes or halls to devise their own courses of study.

Activity 11.3

Find out and compare the aims and courses available from the WEA, Learning Skills Council, Lifelong Learning UK and the University of the Third Age.

Activity 11.4

The International Journal for Lifelong Education may be accessible through your university's library resources. Along with similar journals on comparative education, it explores the principles and practice of lifelong, adult, continuing, recurrent and initial education and learning in all their settings. Sample it to get a sense of the themes that are common across cultures, including the interplay between active citizenship, personal fulfilment, employability and economic development. Another accessible journal is Widening Participation and Lifelong Learning – www.staffs.ac.uk/journal/

Conclusion

Education beyond schools, lifelong learning, education over the lifecourse, all these exciting, visionary yet imprecise terms acknowledge that, as never before, learning is now much more than schooling. It is a habit of mind, essential for economic and spiritual survival. As Sutherland and Crowther put it, 'global economic processes, environmental disasters, terrorism, insecurity at work and the geo-politics of conflict have heightened our sense of uncertainty and of being trapped by forces we know little about and which seem beyond our control' (2006: 3). These authors propose the need for a 'lifelong learning imagination' a process by which we each understand our personal circumstances and the habits of mind, knowledge and skills we possess, an imagination that will enable us as individuals to grow as society shifts all around us and to seize every opportunity to educate ourselves. This is perhaps the real message of the discourse of lifelong learning.

Summary

- the meaning of education has changed as ideas of lifelong learning have taken hold globally
- economic as well as social pressures are shaping the learning society, interpreted through government action in the United Kingdom as in every other country
- currents of learning that have brought us to this point have been outlined
- the archetype of the educated person was explored as it might be essential for the health of any society. The widening participation movement in higher education can be a lever for social justice, efficiency and mobility
- purposeful learning exists in cultures other than the United Kingdom
- lifelong learning is a state of mind, an 'imagination' to which we all must subscribe

References

Allen, E and Storan, J (2005) *Widening Participation: A Rough Guide for Higher Education Providers.* Bradford: Action on Access

Anderson, R (1992) *Universities and Elites in Britain Since 1800.* Basingstoke: Macmillan / Economic History Society

Aspin, D (2007) 'The ontology of values and values education', in Aspin, D and Chapman, J (eds), *Values Education and Lifelong Learning.* Dordrecht: Springer

Brennan, J, Little, B and Locke, W (2006) 'Higher education's effects on disadvantaged groups and communities', Centre for Higher Education Research and Information, the Open University

Coldstream, P (2003) 'Engagement: an unfolding debate', in Bjarnason, S and Coldstream, P (eds), *The Idea of Engagement: Universities and Society.* London: Association of Commonwealth Universities

CEU (Commission of the European Communities) (2000) Memorandum on lifelong learning, Commission Staff Working Paper, Brussels

CEU (Council of the European Union) (2001) 'Report from Education Council on the concrete future objectives of education and training systems', 5980/01. Educ 23. Brussels: CEU

Delors, J et al. (2007) 'Learning: the treasure within: report to UNESCO of the International WORKING Group on Education for the Twenty-first century', Available at: www.unesco.org/delors/delors_e.pdf (accessed 26 October 2007)

Department for Education and Skills (2003) 'The future of higher education', White paper Cm5735. London: HMSO

Drucker, P (1993) *Post-capitalist Society.* Oxford: Butterworth-Heinemann

Dryden, G and Vos, J (2005) *The New Learning Revolution: How Britain Can Lead the World in Learning, Education and Schooling.* London: Continuum

Edwards, R (1997) *Changing Places? Flexibility, Lifelong Learning and a Learning Society.* London: Routledge

Edwards, R, Ranson, S and Strain, M (2002) 'Reflexivity: towards a theory of lifelong learning', *International Journal of Lifelong Education,* 21(6), 525–36

Faure, E, Herrera, F, Kaddoura, A, Petrovsky, A, Rahnenla, M and Ward, F (1972) 'Learning to be: the world of education today and tomorrow', Paris: UNESCO International Commission on the Development of Education

Field, J (2005) *Social Capital and Lifelong Learning.* London: Polity Press

Field, J (2006) *Lifelong Learning and the New Educational Order.* Stoke: Trentham

Fryer, R (1997) Learning for the Twenty-First Century: First Report of the National Advisory Group for Continuing Education and *Lifelong Learning.* London: National Advisory Group for Continuing Education and Lifelong Learning

HECSU (2007) Futuretrack: http://www.hecsu.ac.uk/hecsu.rd/futuretrack_196.htm

Illich, I (1970) *Deschooling Society.* New York: Harper & Row

Istance, D, Schuetze, H and Schuller, T (eds) (2002) *International Perspectives on Lifelong Learning: From Recurrent Education to the Knowledge Society.* Buckingham: Open University Press

Kennedy, H (1997) 'Learning works: widening participation in further education', Coventry, the Further Education Funding Council

Kinder, K, Wakefield, A and Wilkin, A (1996) *Talking Back: Pupil Views on Disaffection.* Slough. NFER

Learning and Skills Council (2007) www.lsc.gov.uk/ (accessed 31 October 2007)

Leitch, S (2006) 'Review of skills: prosperity for all in the global economy: world class skills', final report. London: HM Treasury

Levinson, B, Foley, D and Holland, D (eds) (1996) *The Cultural Production of the Educated Person: Critical Ethnographies of Schooling and Local Practice.* Albany: University of New York Press

Midwinter, E (2004) *500 Beacons: The U3A Story.* London: Third Age Press

NCIHE (National Committee of Inquiry into Higher Education) (1997) *Higher Education in the Learning Society: Report of the National Committee.* London: NCIHE

OECD (Organisation for Economic Cooperation and Development) (1973) *Recurrent Education: A Strategy for Lifelong Learning.* Paris: CERI/OECD

OECD (Organisation for Economic Cooperation and Development) (2004) *Lifelong Learning: Policy Brief.* Paris

OECD (Organisation for Economic Cooperation and Development) (2007) *Education at a Glance: OECD Indicators.* Available at: www.oecd.org/dataoecd/4/55/39313286.pdf (accessed 26 October 2007)

Readings, W (1997) *The University in Ruins.* London: Harvard University Press

Reay, D, David, M and Ball, S (2005) *Degrees of Choice: Social Class, Race and Gender in Higher Education.* London: Trentham

Reimer, E (1971) *School is Dead.* Harmondsworth: Penguin Education

Schuetze, H (2006) 'International concepts and agendas of lifelong learning', *Compare,* 36(3), 289–306

Selwyn, N and Gorard, S (2003) 'Exploring the "new" imperatives of technology-based lifelong learning', *Research in Post-Compulsory Education,* 8(1), 73–92

Sutherland, P and Crowther, J (2006) 'Introduction: the "lifelong learning imagination"', in Sutherland, P and Crowther, J (eds), *Lifelong Learning: Concepts and Contexts.* London: Routledge

UCAS (Universities and Colleges Admissions Service) (2007) 'University and college applicants up 5.2% for 2007', Available at: www.ucas.ac.uk/new/press/news250407.html (accessed 29 June 2007)

Watts, M and Bridges, D (2006) 'The value of non-participation in higher education', *Journal of Education Policy*, 21(3), 267–90

Wolf, A (2002) *Does Education Matter? Myths about Education and Economic Growth*. London: Penguin

Workers' Educational Association (2007) www.wea.org.uk/ (accessed 31 October 2007)

Further reading

Baveye, P (2008) 'Designing university courses to promote lifelong learning', *International Journal of Innovation and Learning*, 5(4), 378–93. This suggests how a course might look if it were specifically designed to prepare you for a life of sustained self-directed learning

Evans, N (2003) *Making sense of Lifelong Learning*. London: RoutledgeFalmer. This has strong sections relating lifelong learning to Widening Participation

Useful websites

Apart from those websites mentioned in the text above, useful stable sources include:

www.dius.gov.uk/ – The Department for Innovation, Universities and Skills (DIUS) sees its work on further and higher education, innovation, science and technology, intellectual property, and supporting evidence-based policy-making as essential to national prosperity because success in a rapidly changing world will only come 'if we develop the skills of our people to the fullest possible extent, carry out world class research and scholarship, and apply both knowledge and skills to create an innovative and competitive economy'.

www.infed.org/ – This site 'exploring informal education, lifelong learning and social action' has updated articles on many of the descriptors of education beyond schools.

www.lluk.org/ittreforms/2760.htm – Lifelong Learning UK is the sector skills council for staff working in the sector. This gives a strong sense of the opportunities in this field and the qualifications now needed to work in it.

Useful search terms

Key words from this chapter will guide you towards sites giving a sense of this fast-moving area:

active learning
continuing education
extended education
informal education
the learning age
the learning rich and the learning poor
life-wide learning
purposeful learning
personalized learning
widening participation and access
workplace learning

Index